Student Affairs for Academic Administrators

ACPA Books and Media Contact Information

ACPA International Office

Tricia A. Fechter Gates
Deputy Executive Director
One Dupont Circle, NW, Suite 300
Washington, DC 20036-1110
(202) 759-4825
FAX (202) 827-0601
pfechter@acpa.nche.edu

ACPA Books and Media

Diane Cooper, Editor
Professor
University of Georgia
402 Aderhold Hall
Athens, GA 30602
dlcooper@uga.edu

Florence M. Guido, Editor
Professor
University of Northern Colorado
Campus Box 103
Greeley, CO 80639
flo.guido@unco.edu

Student Affairs for Academic Administrators

Edited by
T. LYNN HOGAN

ACPA
College Student
Educators International

1996–2016   20ᵀᴴ ANNIVERSARY

STYlus
PUBLISHING, LLC.

STERLING, VIRGINIA

Published by Stylus Publishing, LLC.
22883 Quicksilver Drive
Sterling, Virginia 20166-2102

Library of Congress Cataloging-in-Publication Data
Names: Hogan, T. Lynn, editor.
Title: Student affairs for academic administrators /
edited by T. Lynn Hogan. |
Description: First edition. |
Sterling, Virginia : Stylus Publishing, LLC, 2016. |
Includes bibliographical references and index.
Identifiers: LCCN 2016025818 (print) |
LCCN 2016038966 (ebook) |
ISBN 9781620365717 (casebound : alk. paper) |
ISBN 9781620365724 (pbk. : alk. paper) |
ISBN 9781620365731 (library networkable e-edition) |
ISBN 9781620365748 (consumer e-edition) |
Subjects: LCSH: Student affairs services. |
College student development programs. |
Education, Higher--Administration.
Classification: LCC LB2342.9 .S77 2016 (print) |
LCC LB2342.9 (ebook) | DDC 378.3--dc23
LC record available at https://lccn.loc.gov/2016025818

13-digit ISBN: 978-1-62036-571-7 (cloth)
13-digit ISBN: 978-1-62036-572-4 (paperback)
13-digit ISBN: 978-1-62036-573-1 (library networkable e-edition)
13-digit ISBN: 978-1-62036-574-8 (consumer e-edition)

Printed in the United States of America

All first editions printed on acid-free paper
that meets the American National Standards Institute
Z39-48 Standard.

Bulk Purchases

Quantity discounts are available for use in workshops and for staff
development.
Call 1-800-232-0223

First Edition, 2017

10   9   8   7   6   5   4   3   2   1

In memory of
Dr. Audrey L. Rentz
1941–2010
Major professor, mentor, and friend

Contents

    R<small>ESEARCH AND</small> C<small>REATIVE</small> A<small>CTIVITIES</small>   119
       Korine Steinke Wawrzynski

    About the Contributors   137

    Index   143

Preface

WHEN I WAS IN graduate school at Bowling Green State University in the early 1990s, classroom and colleague conversations often referenced the "gap" between faculty and student affairs professionals. We bemoaned the seeming inability of the two groups to collaborate. Furthermore, we, as student affairs professionals, believed that faculty did not respect our contributions to higher education and to student learning.

Upon graduation, I found myself on the academic side of the house as director of student services for the College of Family and Consumer Sciences at the University of Georgia. In that role and in the 20 years since, I have applied my knowledge of student development theory and student affairs within academic units to further the outcomes for students. My efforts include developing cocurricular programs, consulting on curriculum development, and supporting faculty as they deal with student challenges. Recently, I have worked with faculty members navigating the changing tides of Title IX and accreditation. In addition, academic colleagues have invited me into conversations centered on program reviews, student evaluations, and even faculty development. These invitations into arenas typically ascribed to faculty and academic administrators are based not on personality or "being liked" but rather on recognition of what I, as a student affairs professional, bring to the dialogue.

My experience runs counter to the wisdom we graduate students asserted over coffee while sitting at Grounds for Thought. There is a seat at the academic affairs table for student affairs work. But why is that seat difficult to achieve, and what is preventing greater engagement?

I have come to believe that the gap is really a difference between the cultures of academic affairs and student affairs. There is not some inherent divide to be crossed. Rather, the different perspectives are natural outcomes of experience and, as a result, the gap can be addressed through education and conversation.

For student affairs practitioners, professional development frequently entails completion of a graduate program in college student personnel, higher education, or some similarly named program. These individuals come to graduate school to learn how to holistically develop students in the collegiate milieu through the use of development theory. Graduates understand the theoretical constructs and have experience in applying these ideas to facilitate purposeful student growth through assistantships and practicums. In other words, these student affairs professionals have demonstrated expertise in student development theory and have applied this expertise within the collegiate environment.

Typically, the career path for academic administrators varies significantly from that of their student affairs counterparts. Like student affairs professionals, academic administrators have completed graduate programs. However, unless they completed advanced work in psychology, social work, higher education, or some other related field, they have had little to no exposure to the concepts of working with students beyond classroom teaching and individualized research or study. As students, these professionals focused on developing a deep understanding of a chosen field and an associated research agenda to further knowledge within a specialized arena.

As graduate students, academic administrators may have taught undergraduate courses, hopefully under the guidance of a senior faculty member. This mentorship was most likely the limit of the future administrator's purposeful exposure to working with students. The remainder of the future administrator's understanding probably evolved through interactions with faculty members and observations of interactions between faculty members and other students. Upon graduation, potential academic administrators are experts within their chosen field with perhaps some understanding of how to teach students their subject matter.

After graduation, the student affairs professional assumes a position on a college campus and begins to apply his expertise. Although the associated career may lack a concrete, codified progression, if successful, he may advance to become a director, a dean of students, or a chief student affairs officer. Career advancement for him is based on success in employing his understanding of student development theory and higher education.

For the academic administrator, however, the career path and associated expectations are typically significantly different. Upon graduation, she hopes to secure a faculty or postdoctoral position. With some exceptions, her advancement will rest on success in three areas: research, teaching, and service. Institutional emphasis on the three areas will vary. A faculty member at

Institution A is promoted and tenured for excelling as a researcher and teacher, whereas promotion and tenure criteria at Institution B emphasize teaching and public services. Regardless of the emphasis, these systems traditionally define *teaching* as in-classroom instruction with limited consideration for cocurricular activities.

Like the director of a student affairs unit or the dean of students, the academic affairs administrator typically demonstrates success within the traditionally prescribed system. She probably, though not exclusively, ascended through the faculty ranks of assistant professor, associate professor, and professor. Along the way, she demonstrated administrative abilities and, perhaps, was a good teacher and student mentor. Because of these successes, she might decide that a career in administration is preferable, or perhaps colleagues tap her for departmental leadership responsibility.

Irrespective of the avenues academic administrators and student affairs professionals ultimately take to their respective positions, the fact remains that the two have refined different skill sets and approaches to working with students and, most likely, possess differing expectations of student success. Neither party is right or wrong. Instead, the two groups simply view the purpose and outcomes of a college education differently.

There is a lack not only of a shared academic heritage but also of a shared perception of the role of student affairs in the education of students. As noted previously, student affairs practitioners typically come to their positions with a studied understanding of student affairs and its role on campus. In addition to developmental theory, preparation for these educators encompasses exploration of the basic functions traditionally assigned to student affairs, the role of student affairs in higher education, the philosophy behind the profession, the ethical considerations, and the profession's history. As a result of this education process, practitioners possess a clear and detailed view of the role of student affairs and student affairs functions.

Unless the academic administrator has risen through the ranks of college student personnel or higher education programs, it is unlikely she has had in-depth training in the topics enumerated in the previous paragraph. In all likelihood, she interacted with student affairs while a student, and those interactions shaped her conceptualization of how student affairs units look and function.

This experience-based perception means that the academic administrator who interacted with Greek life, career development, and student activities as a student will likely possess a construct different from that of the person whose major interactions were limited to student conduct, counseling services, and student recreation. In these instances, individual assessment of the value and role of student affairs as a whole is affected by her evaluation of the quality of the interactions with specific units.

Because academic administrators and student affairs professionals approach student affairs from different perspectives, one can anticipate expectations of the purpose and the valuing of these functions to vary significantly. One audience bases its construct on a mixture of personal experience and academic study, whereas the other sees student affairs mostly through an experiential lens.

Given the differences in professional development and understanding of student affairs, it is not surprising that cultural differences exist between the academic affairs and student affairs administrators regarding the purpose and role of student affairs as a member of an education community. Perspectives drive expectations and goals. Without a common foundation, it is difficult to develop a shared language or shared expectations. As a result, collaboration and cooperation can be exceedingly difficult.

However, as higher education faces increased scrutiny around such areas as tuition costs, efficiency, student learning, and graduate employability, it is imperative that institutions effectively deploy all available resources. Because academic administrators typically head higher education institutions, it is incumbent on them to work with colleagues around campus to create high-impact programs producing significant student learning. Student affairs is an ideal place to look for partners.

Student Affairs for Academic Administrators is intended to provide the background and understanding to assist academic administrators in using one important campus resource: student affairs. This book was conceived to provide academic administrators, both new and seasoned, with a fundamental understanding of student affairs as a discipline and a profession. In addition, it highlights traditional academic affairs functions that can be easily adapted to promote student development along other dimensions beyond subject matter expertise. By providing a common foundation, the contributors hope to facilitate communication and collaboration between academic administrators and their student affairs colleagues.

In her insightful introduction Jeanne Gunner, a seasoned academic administrator, articulates the existing landscape of working relationships between academic affairs and student affairs administrators. She enumerates historical and philosophical barriers and contextualizes them by reflecting on her personal frustrations and triumphs. Her firsthand story probably resounds with many academic administrators.

In chapter 1, Holley A. Belch and Amber Racchini provide an overview of the history of student affairs, its basic philosophies, and the functions typically associated with student affairs divisions. The chapter familiarizes academic affairs administrators with the foundational principles and practices of student affairs as a profession. In chapter 2, Ellen M. Broido summarizes current thinking and research in student development theory. Readers will gain an understanding of the theoretical constructs underlying contemporary student affairs practice, as well as explore potential ways to employ these theories in academic administration. In chapter 3, Nancy J. Evans and James DeVita explore diversity issues and how such differences impact student outcomes in the collegiate environment.

Chapter 4 marks the volume's shift to application. Academic affairs professionals interested in greater interaction with student affairs have the following basic options: (a) collaborating with student affairs colleagues and (b) employing the principles in the development of programs wholly contained within academic affairs. In chapter 4, Adrianna Kezar outlines ways to build successful interactions between the two campus communities. In chapter 5, Jennifer Buchanan builds on the concepts outlined by Kezar to frame academic honor codes as a means of collaboration that furthers student moral and ethical development. Finally, in chapter 6, Korine Steinke Wawrzynski discusses how undergraduate research programs can be employed to develop students beyond the intellectual dimension. Chapter 5 highlights collaboration, whereas chapter 6 demonstrates how a traditional academic program can employ student development practices to advance students along multiple dimensions.

Student Affairs for Academic Administrators is for the academic administrator who finds himself or herself in an administrative role that encompasses duties beyond those traditional faculty responsibilities of teaching, research, and service, such as oversight of admissions, advising, student leadership, academic honor codes, honors programs, student organizations, undergraduate research, and national fellowships. Although these programs stress intellectual development, they impact other developmental dimensions as well. This book provides assistance to the administrator seeking to capitalize on such growth opportunities, whether launching a new initiative or seeking to revitalize an existing program.

Student Affairs for Academic Administrators can be a valuable tool for student affairs professionals seeking to establish or reinforce ties with academic colleagues. Student affairs has a shared heritage, philosophy, and theoretical construct. The profession brings significant resources to the table. However, communicating that fact has not been a habit for many in the field. This book might allow for an easier transmission of that information and, as a result, facilitate the opportunity to educate academic colleagues and engage them in discussions surrounding student development.

Ultimately, *Student Affairs for Academic Administrators* is a primer about student affairs as a profession, a discipline, and a campus partner. It is an introduction that contributes to a common language and the formulation of programs that benefit students holistically.

T. Lynn Hogan
Editor

Acknowledgments

A PROJECT LIKE THIS one is not accomplished without support and encouragement from a host of individuals. I want to take this opportunity to say "thank you" to those individuals who helped make *Student Affairs for Academic Administrators* a reality.

I have to begin by saying "thank you" to the American College Personnel Association (ACPA): College Student Educators International and its members for supporting the mechanism through which the manuscript emerged. Working with the Books and Media Board (BAM) has been a great pleasure. They truly demonstrated commitment to working with first-time authors and editors. The advice and encouragement I received was invaluable. In particular, I want to express my gratitude to three individuals. Holley A. Belch, in addition to contributing a chapter, encouraged me throughout the process. Her thoughts at the outset greatly influenced the final product. Denise Collins' guidance was greatly appreciated as the manuscript took shape. Finally, a big thank-you to Kimberly Yousey-Elsener for her support as the book went through the final stage. Thank you all for putting up with the countless and, I am sure at times, inane questions. The process has been a great experience for me.

I want to say "thank you" to Victor Wilson and T. W. Cauthen for providing advice on some of the author selections. Your suggestions were right on the money.

To the authors who contributed to the volume, thank you for trusting me with your work and for bearing with me through the process. I consider it a great honor to have worked with each of you.

The generosity of my home institution, Florida State University (FSU), made this work possible. This book started as part of a sabbatical, and I have enjoyed support throughout the adventure. A special thank-you goes out to Michele, Barbara, Eddie, Sara, Diane, Gabby, and Cassandra for being so competent that I had time to work on the project and not continually worry about office operations. I also want to express my gratitude to Dr. Sally McRorie for encouraging me throughout the writing of this book and for understanding my occasional preoccupations with things other than the job. I appreciate your support and friendship. Also, thank you to Heesung Kim, my great graduate assistant, for preparing the initial index for the book.

As part of my FSU thanks, a special recognition goes to Dr. Robin Leach who took time out of retirement to serve as an editor and proofreader. Her input was invaluable and ensured that the volume was current and relevant. To my friend and colleague, Brad, I also extend a special thank-you for the time you spent helping me process my thoughts and for your continued encouragement.

Finally, I want to say "thank you" to my family for always believing in me and reminding me that I could complete this undertaking. Thank you to Robin not only for reviewing the text but also putting up with me for the past few years as it took its final shape. You are the best!

Introduction

Changing Terrains, Changing Identities

HE OFFICIAL DOCUMENTS OF university life—catalogs, schedules of classes, and websites for orientation, advising, residential learning communities, departments, student organizations, deans' offices, and so on—often appear on paper and in cyberspace as meticulously detailed, comprehensive explanations of the functions of each area, a mapping of defined, discrete territories that appear to work to a holistic end. A world map, too, provides an apparently static set of borders within which each nation-state attends to its business even as it helps compose a global sphere. But the map, as they say, is most certainly not the terrain.

It is unusual for a catalog to do more than descriptively connect academic and student life, and for decades the differing tribes have been free to operate in isolationist fashion. As professionals we should not be surprised to discover, then, that we occupy the university or college spatially tracked—citizens of an imagined whole but experiencing that whole from a largely exclusive perspective as faculty, academic administration, or student affairs leaders—with little information or thought about how our holistic connection is to come about. Within self-contained units, after all, the defining lines and agenda seem clear. "This is an academic institution," says the faculty member; "I am at its center." "This is a place where students develop," says the student affairs professional; "We must see to their growth." "This place is inefficiently run," says the academic affairs administrator; "Policies and procedures must be implemented." The worldviews don't just fail to align; the disjunctions also obscure any clear perception of how each area is part of a whole.

1

With the current paradigm-shifting changes to higher education nationally and internationally, however, the conventional academic attitudes toward student affairs of live-and-let-live or need-to-know forms of contact are being upended. Assessment and reaccreditation reviews, marketing and competition for student bodies, experiential learning initiatives, retention and graduation rate scrutiny, and internship and vocational pressures all combine to induce formerly coexisting tribes to new forms of interaction and cooperation. Student affairs and academic affairs increasingly exist in dynamic relation, and each is affected by greater social changes in the fast-paced environment of higher education's economic and demographic change. This necessary move from benign segregation to productive partnership requires that we engage in some identity renegotiation.

In this introduction, I work toward identifying some of the cultural value differences that can occur (and perhaps typify more of a historical record than a current reflection) in the academic affairs–student affairs connection. Ultimately, though, I argue for the necessity and value of partnership and the exploration of common ground. By acknowledging and foregrounding the shared imperatives of academic affairs and student affairs, we have much improved the odds of creating useful programs and policies and the trust required for dissolving them as they no longer apply (for all indicators suggest that the higher education environment for the foreseeable future remains enormously dynamic). Being part of strategic alliances is the more productive mode of connection.

The benefits of academic affairs–student affairs partnering on a wide range of areas and activities are obvious from the extensive research data on student learning and retention from massive surveys such as the National Survey of Student Engagement to careful analyses of them by scholars such as George D. Kuh, Ernest T. Pascarella, and Patrick T. Terenzini, as well as Ernest Boyer. Furthermore, in light of the embarrassing findings published in Richard Arum and Josipa Roksa's (2011) *Academically Adrift* or Rebekah Nathan's (2005) ethnographic *My Freshman Year*, we might expect a growing fusion of holistic approaches to student success to be necessary and efficacious. With the shift in the very nature of knowledge as it is increasingly pursued and presented in new digital forms, as social media and a technology-saturated cultural environment redefine human relations, and as interdisciplinarity remediates traditional academic specialization, it seems axiomatic that student learning necessarily entails the broader realms of experience that student affairs addresses.

And yet higher education researcher Adrianna Kezar (2003) identified a significant list of major institutional barriers that an academic affairs–student affairs alliance faces:

> organizational fragmentation and division of labor, specialization among faculty, lack of common purpose or language, few shared values, history of separation, different priorities and expectations, cultural differences between academic and student affairs in terms of personality styles, and competing assumptions about what constitutes effective learning. (p. 3)

Her list certainly rings true for me in terms of my own experience (which is admittedly inflected by generational and disciplinary experience, and newer and younger administrators from more relevant fields may not identify). I can say that my initial contacts with the institutional world of student affairs felt quite like visiting a foreign land without a guidebook. Its notions of the academic came at the issues of education in ways I had experienced neither as a student (in a long-gone student-life era that was much more regulatory than developmental) nor as a new faculty member in a large state institution (also decades in the past), whose agenda was more a competitive academic Darwinism than an integrative, whole-person and community-building process. I felt a need to acculturate to a value system different from the classroom or academic meeting, which entailed, I slowly realized, a decentering disruption of my sense of my professional self. I could move across the discourse communities of academic units comfortably, but this was code shifting of a different order. It's no wonder that the former parallel universes of student affairs and academic affairs, rapidly reunifying as they are, still have the trace of some fundamental cultural differences in the form of Kezar's list.

To Kezar's list I would add *professional identities*, manifested as they are by and on professional turf, as a likely complication to smooth cooperation. As student affairs expert Arthur Sandeen (2004) asserted, "Student affairs leaders have expanded their professional interests and reject any suggestion that they are just 'service providers' [but instead] see themselves as an integral part of the academic programs of their campuses and active contributors to student learning" (p. 30). Not just service providers and active contributors— these concepts likely find agreement among those on the academic affairs side. Integral part of the academic programs? That may sometimes be harder to embrace. That's uncomfortably close, for some, to an almost proprietary claim. And it foregrounds the serious question of what *student learning* consists of, as Kezar noted, and of how broad and capacious a definition the

academic conception of it can and should be. If faculty perceive themselves
as the center of an institutional universe, which is in turn perceived as being
necessarily ordered by academic administrators, what space is left for the
student affairs leader? What ground exists to be shared?

The concepts of students and student learning often become the point
of triangulation for the attempt to reframe identities and institutional relationships. The construct of *the student* is central to professional identities in
both student affairs and academic affairs, but its definition and implications
vary to a very significant degree. The student subject in an academic frame
may be the empty vessel Paolo Freire (2007) critiqued or the self-directing
community learner his critical pedagogy promoted, or the student subject
might be interpellated from deficit or merit or from some other relationship
to academic knowledge. The academic identity that is coconstructed may
therefore be the expert, the mentor, the standard-bearer and judge, the critical liberator, or the democratic partner. The power of the persona derives
from an academic knowledge base, and institutional power derives from the
ability to connect an academic agenda to the construct of the student. Academics and academic administrators, in other words, understandably rely on
an academic view of students.

The student affairs student subject, on the other hand, seems more commonly put in relation to a holistic notion of the subject. This subject develops
in texture and hue, with an ultimately stable and knowable identity. From
this perspective, the student is a self-realizing subject. The coconstructed
student affairs professional identity seems, if no longer an *in loco parentis*
persona, a shaping force of a different order. Kuh (2003) outlined the developmental process:

> The engagement premise is deceptively simple, even self-evident: The more
> students study a subject, the more they learn about it. Likewise, the more stu-
> dents practice and get feedback on their writing, analyzing, or problem solv-
> ing, the more adept they become. The very act of being engaged also adds to
> the foundation of skills and dispositions that is essential to live a productive,
> satisfying life after college. That is, students who are involved in educationally
> productive activities in college are developing habits of the mind and heart
> that enlarge their capacity for continuous learning and personal development.
> (p. 25)

As Kuh (2003) argued, a whole-person development agenda includes—
depends on—intellectual growth; academic expertise is not the sole

developmental force, as his developmental schema reflects. Each side works to resolve the Cartesian mind–body split. The embodied student self is a critical concept for academics; the holistic student self is an ethical imperative for student affairs. In ideal form, together they impel a student toward growth as both an independent, self-questioning critical agent and a community-focused peer and leader. The student subject is thus both a critical and an ethical construct.

What all this might mean in material form in academic affairs–student affairs relations today is a willingness to operate increasingly frequently against the traditional grain. A useful example is one of the earliest border-shifting initiatives, which came in the form of residential learning communities (RLC). As in border studies, the focus in such early experimentation was the liminal spaces of experience—the contact in casual environments with conceptual issues in the form of linked classes and housing, residence hall guest speakers, informal faculty–student conversations, and related activities. And as in border studies, what can be seen is the subtle but powerful shifting of roles—a decentering of authority, a relocation of the intellectual sphere, and, ideally, a redefining of self for all parties involved. In the RLC structure, students and faculty came to interact in less hierarchical ways; learning came to be more experiential, not simply in its form but in the perception of its operation—of how one learns and of how one learns in more than conventional books-and-classroom formats. The notion of the social contexts of learning expanded. As Zhao and Kuh (2004) reported

> Participating in learning communities is uniformly and positively linked with student academic performance, engagement in educationally fruitful activities (such as academic integration, active and collaborative learning, and interaction with faculty members), gains associated with college attendance, and overall satisfaction with the college experience. (p. 124)

The frequently cited retention effect of RLCs, while a seemingly inescapable measure in the current environment, can be seen as the bonus, and the cultural shift of expanded and blended learning spaces, real and conceptual, can be seen as the significant outcome.

An institution needn't undertake a massive renovation of residential and learning systems to initiate border-shifting effects, however. In one example of the power of local innovations, I can offer the modest beginnings of our now-united academic affairs–student affairs structure. In the midst of our institution's overhauling of its academic mission, I invited representatives from every student affairs office—orientation, housing, conduct, study abroad, Greek life, counseling, and so on—to form a planning group that would redefine our first-year programs. Many of us had never met each other before, despite our institution's relatively small size. Our initial productivity came in the form of a redefined orientation program (Gunner et al., 2008). More significant, the contact enabled new partnerings (part of the orientation came under the academic events coordinator, for example, encouraging a shared sense of ownership), opened up formerly suppressed topics and disagreements (do the student organizations promote an academic elite, or should they be inclusive?), produced the cited collaborative article, and initiated shifts in responsibility areas (retention programs moved from my office to the dean of students' office) and in the organizational chart (all of these offices are currently under the chancellor). It has been messy, sometimes upsetting, often provocative. It has forced a questioning of identities and a remapping of the academic activities that produce them. Most of all, it has produced an environment in which change is seen as not only sometimes challenging but also always open-ended; change engenders more change, and no organizational chart can determine the terrain of any of us once and for all. We have become multinational. The old borders do not hold, and the new generations are on the way to global citizenship.

Kezar (2003) noted the changes in institutional culture that are most conducive to productive academic affairs–student affairs collaboration:

> Cooperation (73%), student affairs staff attitudes (66%), common goals (63%), and personalities (62%) were believed to make the most difference in the success of collaborative efforts. These strategies are all cultural approaches toward change. In open-ended responses, most people mentioned that new people or new leadership had come to campus, which helped significantly in making the change. (p. 13)

In my experience, the last item is key: New leadership—not necessarily new people—can produce the other effects and can emerge out of current conditions, out of cooperative efforts rather than new hires or new budget lines. But this is not a hierarchical list of most effective strategies, best practices, or other decontextualized prescriptions; Kezar wrote about multiple, often competing, dynamic institutional conditions. Cooperation goes along with attitude changes; common goals emerge from contending personalities: Change, finally, is really the single most productive environmental factor.

We cannot avoid change, and that is a good thing. It happens to us, to the very notion of "I" and "thou," creating an "us." The borders have been breached, and we find ourselves in new, productive relationships, with old identities transformed by new contacts and a new culture emerging from them. It is in this dynamic environment, far more than in a mechanistic, behaviorist, instrumentalist notion of standards, transferability, and seamlessness, that a more than prescriptive sense of new forms of learning and institutional adaptation can disrupt settled but outmoded lines. We need to globalize ourselves, opening up the closed kingdoms of our campuses. The students we teach, in all the manifold forms of teaching, will be the beneficiaries. And we, too, can find in such change new ways of being, acting, and interacting. The assimilation of purposes is not the end of difference but a strengthening of effectiveness in the aims of our shared educational terrain.

Jeanne Gunner
Vice Chancellor and Professor of English, Retired
Chapman University

REFERENCES

Arum, R., & Roksa, J. (2011). *Academically adrift*. Chicago, IL: University of Chicago Press.

Freire, P. (2007). *Pedagogy of the oppressed*. New York, NY: Continuum.

Gunner, J., Branch, S., Harran, M., McNenny, G., Osborn, J., O'Donnell, K., & Robbins, N. (2008). Models of global citizenship: Students and media as/in academic orientation. In M. J. LaBarr (Ed.), *Civic engagement in the first year of college* (pp. 41–43). New York, NY, and Columbia, SC: The New York Times and The National Resource Center.

Kezar, A. (2003). Achieving student success: Strategies for creating partnerships between academic and student affairs. *NASPA, 41*(1), 1–21.

Kuh, G. D. (2003). What we're learning about student engagement from NSSE: Benchmarks for effective educational practices. *Change, 35*(2), 24–32.

Nathan, R. (2005). *My freshman year*. Ithaca, NY: Cornell University Press.

Sandeen, A. (2004). Educating the whole student: The growing academic importance of student affairs. *Change, 36*(3), 28–33.

Zhao, C.-M., & Kuh, G. D. (2004). Adding value: Learning communities and student engagement. *Research in Higher Education, 45*(2), 115–138.

Part One

Understanding the Field and Its Foundations

LIKE MANY PROFESSIONS, THE student affairs field possesses shared heritage and foundational constructs that guide its practice. This first part of *Student Affairs for Academic Administrators* serves as a primer on the profession. The authors explore its history, functions, and underlying theories and the role diversity plays in its practices.

The fundamentals presented in these chapters provide academic affairs administrators with the language and level of understanding needed to maximize collaborations with student affairs colleagues. In addition, this material is intended to motivate academic administrators to consider how student development theories and student affairs practices might be integrated into traditionally academic undertakings to enhance the student learning experience.

1

Student Affairs

A Primer

Holley A. Belch and Amber Racchini

UNDERSTANDING STUDENT AFFAIRS PROFESSIONALS and the basic philosophical assumptions of their work on college campuses is connected with the development of American higher education. The context of higher education and the evolution of faculty influenced the development of student affairs, and, subsequently, the context of student affairs has helped to shape the experiences students have in college.

HISTORICAL CONTEXT

As higher education emerged in the seventeenth century, colonial America sought to emulate the English residential college model. Gentlemen scholars characterized young men attending the colonial colleges where the classics, character development, the refinement of civilized graces, and religious instruction were emphasized (Thelin, 2004). A few faculty and the president were responsible for all aspects of student lives outside the classroom, including cocurricular, moral, athletic, and social activities (Dungy & Gordon, 2011; Hirt, 2006). These college officials acted *in loco parentis*, or in place of parents, as they constructed a highly structured authoritarian environment for students dictated by religious doctrine.

By the mid eighteenth century, however, the nature of the higher education student began to evolve. The decline of religion as the mainstay of education gave way to the expansion of curriculum and the development of the elective system (Rudolph, 1990; Thelin, 2004). This shift in focus altered the type of student who enrolled (Dungy & Gordon, 2011; Hirt, 2006). One characteristic of this population change was that the stringent rules and regulations of early colleges alienated many students from faculty and campus officials (Brubacher & Rudy, 2004). Student discontent was evident as demonstrations and acts of defiance and rebellion occurred (Thelin, 2004).

Students sought ways to express themselves and engage with one another outside of the classroom. Although early student organizations focused on academic pursuits (e.g., literary societies, debating clubs), more socially oriented student groups (e.g., fraternities, secret societies) soon appeared (Rudolph, 1990; Thelin, 2004). A student culture emerged on campuses that would have significant influence as students found satisfaction in the discussions and activities beyond the formal classroom (Rudolph, 1990). These student organizations (including fraternities and sororities) frequently shared a common residence off campus away from the oversight of college officials. Over time, these activities attracted the scrutiny of college officials who sought to control or tried to formalize the activity, with mixed results (Thelin, 2004). Consequently, regulating student housing and conduct issues emerged as a challenge for campus officials (Bogue & Aper, 2000).

CHANGING FACULTY ROLE

Although the nature of the residential model changed, the nature of faculty was evolving as well. During the nineteenth century, the growth of scientific knowledge, secularization of American society, and subsequent demise of the classical curriculum gave way to the development of academic disciplines, specialization, and the demand for advanced graduate training among faculty (Rudolph, 1990; Schuster & Finkelstein, 2011). Nineteenth-century faculty were more experienced, were considered professional educators, and had advanced degrees (Schuster & Finkelstein, 2011). With the expansion and growing complexity of higher education, the notion of permanent faculty eventually displaced the original tutor model. College presidents and faculty reassessed their roles in the student experience as the emphasis grew on research and scholarship for faculty and student interest in developing the out-of-class experience (Dungy & Gordon, 2011).

By the second half of the nineteenth century, the traditional classical college transformed, and the diversity of higher education began to take shape. In the final decades of the nineteenth century, an expanding and changing student population combined with a growing variety of institutions forced colleges and universities to change their day-to-day operations (Schwartz, 2002). The increasing complexity of the president's role, coupled with a shift in faculty culture to pursue research-oriented endeavors rather than noninstructional activities necessitated hiring administrative staff to coordinate and oversee areas such as admissions, registration, student discipline, housing, student activities, and student health (Brubacher & Rudy, 2004; Hirt, 2006; Rhatigan, 2009). "As American campuses increasingly exhibited both an active social culture and an emphasis on intellectual goals, individuals were needed who could specialize in integrating the two so that the social aspects did not overgrow the academic mission" (Gerda, 2004, p. 19).

THE FORMAL EMERGENCE OF STUDENT AFFAIRS

The presence of women on college campuses brought the need for someone to oversee the needs and concerns of female students. By the 1890s, the role of *dean of women* began appearing formally on coeducational campuses (Brubacher & Rudy, 2004; Gerda, 2004). These deans of women were often faculty members in liberal arts who were deeply concerned about students, well educated and competent, and conveyed a sense of warmth and compassion (Rhatigan, 2009). By the turn of the twentieth century, the *dean of men* position had emerged (Brubacher & Rudy, 2004), partially modeled after the dean of women template (Gerda, 2004). Although position responsibilities varied across institutions and although roles were ill defined, the expectations were that these deans were overseers of student behavior, general welfare, and "the affective dimensions of the student experience" (Rhatigan, 2009, p. 9).

In addition to the deans, student personnel workers (e.g., registrars, vocational counselors, admissions officers, student activity advisers) served a growing and diverse population of students (Rudolph, 1990). Increased enrollment, coupled with the secularization in higher education, recognition of disciplinary expertise, and the more impersonal, intellectual posture emerging in higher education combined to support the student personnel movement in the 1920s (Bogue & Aper, 2000; Rhatigan, 2009; Schuster & Finkelstein, 2011). "The movement established on campuses across the nation an infrastructure designed to address the non-intellectual, nonacademic needs of college students" (Schuster & Finkelstein, 2011, p. 12). The professionalization of the student personnel movement was underway in 1913 as Teachers College, Columbia University was the first to design a graduate program. Professional organizations were subsequently formed. By the 1930s, the American Council on Education (ACE) supported the professional practice of student personnel (Dungy & Gordon, 2011; Rentz & Howard-Hamilton, 2011).

Concurrently, faculty formed learned societies, such as the American Association of University Professors, with associated scholarly journals to serve their professional interests. By the 1930s, the academic committee structure established on campuses affirmed faculty's role in institutional governance, policy making, curriculum, and service, thus setting the stage for the model of contemporary faculty life—teaching, research, and service (Schuster & Finkelstein, 2011). This systematization of faculty priorities cemented the role student personnel had in serving students in American higher education.

ESTABLISHING A PHILOSOPHICAL FOUNDATION

The leaders of the student personnel movement recognized the need to codify and publish their purpose and guiding principles for working with students. Through ACE, they issued a conference report, *The Student Personnel Point of View (SPPV)* (ACE, 1937). An updated and expanded perspective, the *SPPV Revised* (ACE, 1949), was published more than a decade later. These documents form the guiding philosophical foundation of the student affairs profession. Essentially, the 1937 *SPPV* affirmed the basic purposes of higher education (Rhatigan, 2009) and emphasized the development of the student holistically to encompass the person and not solely the intellect (ACE, 1937). The values espoused in the 1937 *SPPV* emphasized assisting students in their intellectual, personal, and moral development and recognized that learning is the result of a compilation of varied experiences both in and outside the classroom. Furthermore, it articulated 23 functions or services essential to successful institutions, advocated for coordination of efforts within and outside of institutions, called for more research on students and graduates, and highlighted a need for national leadership (ACE, 1937).

The 1949 revision reflected societal changes and called for greater understanding and expansion of international programs, added to the identifiable services for students, and advocated for a separate administrative structure for student personnel services. It underscored the individualistic nature of students while acknowledging that students have responsibility in their development and learning (ACE, 1949). Specifically, the 1949 *SPPV* articulated,

> The student personnel movement constitutes one of the most important efforts of American educators to treat the college and university students as individuals, rather than entries in an impersonal roster. . . . In a real sense, this part of modern higher education is an individualized application of the research and clinical findings of modern psychology, sociology, cultural anthropology, and education to the task of aiding students to develop fully in the college environment. (ACE, 1949, para 10)

The functions and services delineated in the *SPPV* (ACE, 1937, 1949) established roles for student personnel workers separate and distinct from that of faculty. The student affairs profession "came into its own" (Hirt, 2006, p. 7) following World War II. The impact of burgeoning enrollments in the postwar era meant more complex admissions policies and procedures and expansion of new classrooms, laboratories, and residential facilities. Perhaps the most compelling effect was that veterans represented a new profile of the American college student: older, married, some with children, and a portion with disabilities (Thelin, 2004). This period also saw increased focus on serving other "new" students (women, ethnic and racial minorities) entering higher education in greater numbers (Rhatigan, 2009).

THE TRANSFORMATION OF STUDENT AFFAIRS: 1960s THROUGH EARLY 1970s

As higher education was evolving, so too was student affairs. During the 1960s, American colleges were prospering and growing, and major cultural events, such as age of majority, the Vietnam War, the women's movement, and the civil rights movement, as well as legal precedent like *Dixon v. Alabama State Board of Education*, which effectively ended the practice of *in loco parentis*, influenced a changing expectation among college students. The doctrine of *in loco parentis* had shaped the student affairs profession and higher education for nearly two centuries. Student activism, unrest, and discontent challenged the paradigm. The role of student affairs practitioners shifted from that of parents to professionals providing programs and services to students (Hirt, 2007). Their role now included acknowledging and, at times, championing students' legal rights (i.e., due process, free speech, and access to educational records). Simultaneously, student advisory boards emerged, and student representation occurred on institutional governing boards and in judicial processes.

Professionalization and Graduate Preparation

As student personnel work began to crystalize and form throughout the first half of the twentieth century, discussions among professional association leadership continued to emphasize the educational and experiential background of student personnel workers. Several prominent leaders recognized that student personnel workers had varied backgrounds and no common core of knowledge. Changing roles and expectations reinforced the movement toward formal education for student affairs administrators (Cowley, 1937; Wrenn, 1959). The Commission on Professional Development of the Council of Student Personnel Associations in Higher Education met to develop recommendations for graduate programs, resulting in a proposal emphasizing three areas of focus: a professional core, areas of inquiry to broaden and deepen the core, and specialty options (e.g., housing, college unions, admissions) through practicum or internship experiences (Emmet & Sheldon, 1965).

New Foundation for Practice

In the late 1960s and early 1970s, the profession called for a new foundational philosophy to anchor work with college students. A new perspective in student affairs, student development theory, emerged as a foundation for practice (see chapter 2) and resulted in a dramatic change for the profession. Student development theory, grounded in human development theory, reemphasized a commitment to the whole student and a call for collaboration between faculty and student affairs to promote student development (R.D. Brown, 1972). These theoretical orientations, drawn from social, organizational, developmental psychology, and counseling fields, offered an understanding of the needs of traditional-age college students, created a common language for practitioners (McEwen, 2003), and changed the very nature of the practitioner role from service provider to developmental and educational facilitator (Hirt, 2007). Consequently, student affairs administrators shed their historical moniker, *student personnel worker*, and openly embraced a new philosophy and role in the campus community. Affirmation of the importance of their role on campus came after many college presidents included the senior student affairs officer in the president's cabinet, often resulting in the presence of the vice president for student affairs (Gaston-Gayles, Wolf-Wendel, Tuttle, Twombly, & Ward, 2005). All of these elements fueled the most prolific growth in master's- and doctoral-level graduate education in this field in the 1960s and 1970s. Two thirds of master's-level programs with identifiable program initiation dates began in the 1960s and 1970s (Coomes & Talbot, 2000; DeSawal, Hornak, & Mueller, 2011).

A TIME OF TURBULENCE: 1970s THROUGH 1990s

Between the 1970s and 1990s, higher education experienced seismic shifts on multiple fronts. National studies chronicled the shortcomings of higher education, fueling skepticism and distrust (Thelin, 2004). Federal mandates such as Section 504 of the Rehabilitation Act and Title IX of the Education Amendments (1972) began to play a larger role in the life of institutions (Manning, Kinzie, & Schuh, 2006; Thelin, 2004). Accountability in the form of retention concerns also emerged during this period (Thelin, 2004).

The nature of students and their expectations also altered during this period. Institutions, particularly public colleges, could no longer count on traditional-age, majority-dominated, residential students in their classrooms (Thelin, 2004). Students from underrepresented groups (e.g., economically challenged, ethnic minorities, first generation, students with disabilities, women) gained increasing access to higher education. Simultaneously, parents and students wanted more from the cocurricular, which gave rise to more formalization of career services offices, health and fitness centers, and the evolution of residence halls to include modern-day amenities (Thelin, 2004). Beyond the physical structural changes in residence halls, coeducational housing emerged, as well as themed housing, which appealed to students with similar interests and, in some cases, connected faculty and the curriculum to the out-of-classroom experience, providing the opportunity for a seamless learning environment.

This confluence of external changes and fluid student demographics further solidified the importance of student affairs professionals to the success of higher education. Student affairs was at the forefront of helping campus leadership adjust to changes precipitated by federal mandates (Manning et al., 2006; Thelin, 2004). Similarly, student affairs professionals helped faculty and academic administrators understand more about new student groups and their needs in the learning environment, often taking the lead in areas such as retention.

Proponents of change in the 1980s also advocated for a restructuring of higher education, moving away from an instructional paradigm rooted in teaching provided solely by faculty to a learning paradigm that focused on educational outcomes and student learning. One such report, *Involvement in Learning: Realizing the Potential of American Higher Education* (Study Group on the Conditions of Excellence in American Higher Education, 1984), highlighted the effects of student involvement and motivation on student learning and acknowledged the positive impact of collaborative partnerships. These ideas resonated with the student affairs profession, supported their existing literature, and initiated self-examination of their role in student learning on college campuses.

STUDENT LEARNING AND STUDENT AFFAIRS: 1990s THROUGH 2010

Since the 1990s, the emerging focus on student learning has underscored the integral role student affairs plays in overall student learning. To foster seamless educational experiences, the emphasis on collaboration between faculty and student affairs professionals has grown (American College Personnel Association [ACPA], 1994; Kuh, 1996). Although colleges and universities were challenged to reexamine the student experience and reemphasize the notion of student learning, several key publications (e.g., Kuh, Schuh, Whitt, & Associates, 1991; Pascarella & Terenzini, 2005) grounded in research affirmed the substantive contributions of the out-of-class experience to student learning and development (Manning et al., 2006). The research demonstrated in a clear and compelling manner that learning is cumulative and results from multiple experiences both in and outside of the established curriculum (Pascarella & Terenzini, 2005). Professional student affairs associations drew attention to the need to focus on student learning (ACPA, 1994) and collaborate with academic affairs (American Association for Higher Education, American College Personnel Association, & National Association of Student Personnel Administrators, 1998). The *Principles of Good Practice* (ACPA & NASPA, 1998) extended the discussion, was rooted in historical documents such as the *SPPV* (ACE, 1937) and the *Student Learning Imperative* (ACPA, 1994), and provided a plan to student affairs divisions for becoming learning oriented. Subsequently, two major professional associations, the American College Personnel Association (ACPA) and the National Association of Student Personnel Administrators (NASPA), collectively outlined the standards for student learning for student affairs and offered recommendations for application and direction for assessment and evaluation (Keeling, 2004, 2006). These calls for reform and responses offered a clear and distinct paradigm shift from the student development model to the student learning model—one grounded in understanding the role student affairs plays in facilitating student learning.

FUNCTIONAL AREAS IN STUDENT AFFAIRS

As noted previously, the 1937 *SPPV* and 1949 revision (ACE, 1937, 1949) identified services or functions (e.g., admissions, financial aid, counseling and testing, orientation, discipline, recreational activities, summer employment, and placement) within student affairs (Sandeen, 2001). Essentially, the *SPPV* "laid the groundwork for functions of student affairs practice" (Manning et al., 2006, p. 5) to evolve into a complex division that provides myriad departments and programs or functional areas.

Factors Influencing the Organization of Student Affairs

The historical development of higher education and student affairs continues to influence its modern-day organization on college campuses. Key factors such as institutional mission, institutional history and tradition, culture and size, professional staff background, student characteristics, financial resources, organizational structure, and institutional leadership all influence how student affairs is organized (Love, Kuh, MacKay, & Hardy, 1993; Sandeen, 2001). In addition, different philosophies about and approaches to student affairs work (i.e., student services, student development, or student learning) affect the organization as well (Manning et al., 2006). Divisional leadership is generally provided by a vice president for student affairs or dean of students who is part of the president's leadership team or may report to the senior academic officer depending on the campus structure.

Description of Functional Areas

To represent broadly the services, departments, and functions commonly associated with student affairs divisions on college campuses, we clustered the functional areas thematically. Not all campuses reflect these departments in student affairs. Unless otherwise noted, these departments are typically organized under a student affairs division. Professionals at larger institutions may have more specialized skills, whereas those at small colleges may have responsibilities that extend beyond a particular functional area.

Academic support and related programs (academic advising, learning assistance programs, disability support services, service-learning). The comprehensive term *academic support* includes departments and services designed to support students in the learning process. The primary mission is to assist students in developing the skills needed to reach their academic and career goals. Some institutions administer fully or in part various academic support components through the student affairs division and may cluster them in an academic support center, which serves as a hub for support services. The services or departments, which fall under the purview of academic support generally, include academic advising, learning assistance programs, disability support services, and service-learning. These centers are a natural venue for collaboration between faculty and student affairs professionals.

Considered a holistic and developmental process, academic advising requires collaboration across divisional boundaries (Campbell, 2008). Multiple advising models (faculty only, professional advisers, combinations) exist, yet they share a common goal of helping students meet their educational, personal, and career goals. The organization of advising on campus is influenced by institutional factors (e.g., institutional control, level of degrees offered, program offerings, selectivity, budget and resources) and student characteristics (e.g., first generation, underprepared, level of diversity), thus creating institution-specific rationales for organization and delivery of services (King, 2008). Regardless of how advising is organized, it needs a connection to a variety of student affairs services (e.g., admissions, orientation, career services, learning communities). On campuses where student affairs is not directly involved in advising, staff can provide valuable assistance in understanding student characteristics and developmental issues and should be included in the professional development of faculty and professional advisers (T. Brown, 2008).

Learning assistance programs such as TRIO (e.g., Upward Bound, Talent Search, Ronald McNair Post-Baccalaureate Achievement Program, Student Support Services) have evolved and expanded over time yet still maintain an original vision of increasing access to and completion of higher education to first-generation, low-income students (Council for Opportunity in Education, 2016). At many institutions, these programs network with existing institutional programs, services, and resources rather than establish separate and distinct components. The direct link is student success, and faculty are often involved in associated recruitment activities, summer bridge programs, and ongoing academic support.

A primary role of disability support services is to provide students with opportunities for success by working with their individual needs. Services typically include reviewing and verifying medical documentation of disability, notifying individual faculty of the accommodations afforded to students enrolled in their courses, working with students with disabilities on self-advocacy skills, coordinating services (i.e., note taking, interpreters), and providing testing accommodations. Standard academic support services (e.g., time management skills, tutoring, study skills techniques) may also be part of a disability support service (Colwell, 2006).

Service-learning can serve as a curricular partnership between student affairs and academic affairs (Kezar, 2009). Linking credit-bearing course content to community service, coupled with a reflection component, helps students acquire new skills, values, and knowledge through the integration of classroom curriculum and hands-on learning experience (Kuh & Hinkle, 2002). Student affairs professionals can provide logistical support to faculty by establishing relationships with local community-service agencies, provide reflection training sessions, assist with grant applications, and assist in developing and evaluating service-learning projects for students to complete (Dale & Drake, 2005; Kezar, 2009).

Campus activities (student activities, college unions, conferences and events, Greek affairs, leadership development, recreational programs, and community service). Campus activities represent the out-of-class, cocurricular programs provided to support student growth and development along multiple dimensions (social, academic, physical, spiritual, emotional, and professional) (Whipple & O'Neill, 2011). The primary goal is to complement the academic mission of the institution by enhancing the overall educational experience of students through planning and implementing social, cultural, intellectual, recreational, and leadership programs (Whipple & O'Neill, 2011).

Although there is no prescribed way to administer student activities, it is imperative to consider the characteristics of the institution's student population when developing programming (Whipple & O'Neill, 2011). Regardless of institutional size or oversight of programs, creating learning opportunities that extend beyond the classroom is paramount to maximizing student development.

Faculty involvement is essential in creating purposeful opportunities that connect directly with in-class learning. Collaboration with campus activities may include providing input on the development of a speaker or film series, requiring students to attend a campus lecture series, providing ideas for films or other media, advising student organizations (academic or personal interest), hosting meetings or out-of-class activities in the student union, or facilitating a student leadership conference workshop. Large-scale coordination of programs and resources between the provost and the vice president for student affairs can maximize efforts and resources and minimize scheduling conflicts on campus, which is particularly important at small colleges.

Enrollment management (admissions, financial aid, orientation, and career services). Emerging in the late twentieth century, *enrollment management* is defined broadly as a means of organizing a series of interrelated services on college campuses with the goal of influencing the characteristics or size of student enrollments. This objective is attainable through activities focused on student choice, the transition to college, attrition and retention, and educational outcomes, all rooted in strategic planning and institutional research (Hossler, 2011). Organizationally, a senior-level administrator has authority over a number of central areas (e.g., admissions, orientation, career services, financial aid), with a system-wide approach based on communication, cooperation, and resource allocation (Hossler, 2011). On campuses where student retention or student outcomes research is the responsibility of student affairs, enrollment management naturally falls within the student affairs division (Hossler, 2011).

Since the 1970s, admissions offices have focused on using marketing techniques to increase exposure to and attract more students (Hossler, 2011). More sophisticated analysis of student characteristics, student choice in attending the institution, student attrition and retention data, and student outcomes help ensure that institutions are recruiting students who are a good fit for the institution and who will enroll, be retained, and ultimately graduate (Hossler, 2011). Although the quality and reputation of faculty members, coupled with the major and program offerings, determine where students attend college, it is imperative that students appreciate academic and social norms, faculty, and the physical layout of the campus to ensure the aforementioned fit (Hossler, 2011).

The purpose of financial aid is multifaceted; beyond access and equity to education, the goals include influencing students to pursue academic areas that meet labor shortages, acknowledging and rewarding service to the country, and remedying past injustices (McPherson & Schapiro, as cited in

Hossler, 2000). Financial aid is linked directly with enrollment decisions and retention where the challenge often is determining the effects of price or cost of education on the availability of financial aid (Hossler, 2000). Ultimately, though, federal and state regulations direct this area's mission and purpose (Haynes & Bush, 2011).

Responsibilities include administering financial aid programs (i.e., loan, grant, campus based), monitoring institutional compliance and student eligibility, counseling students, determining financial need, and working with various campus constituencies (Haynes & Bush, 2011). A financial aid department may report to an enrollment management organization or may align with student affairs given the central role it plays in retention. In some institutions, a business services model may align financial aid with fiscal affairs (Haynes & Bush, 2011).

Programs orienting new students to college have existed on campuses since the late nineteenth century. However, modern programs have evolved, have become more comprehensive, and are directly related to retention strategies (Overland, Rentz, & Sarnicki, 2011). An orientation program focuses on providing a seamless and successful transition from high school to college, or from one institution to another in the case of transfer students, and introduces parents and families to the student's college experience and the expected partnership with the institution.

More recently, orientation programs have adopted an academic focus to assist students with both social and academic integration (Overland et al., 2011). A variety of program models exist (one day, two day, weekend, the week prior to the start of classes, or yearlong), characterized by an equally diverse array of programs (adventure programs, learning communities, courses, bridge programs, summer reading, online or web based) offered in either a credit or a noncredit format (Overland et al., 2011). Common program elements across institutions may include placement testing, advising and course registration, campus tours, information sessions, and opportunities for social interaction with other new and returning students. Recognizing the differing needs of student populations and designing programs accordingly are critically important. Within this context, there are multiple opportunities for involvement of faculty and others on campus, including, for example, participation in the long-term planning efforts, involvement with a summer reading requirement, participation in orientation advising sessions, and general activities.

The goal of a career services office is to help guide students in envisioning, creating, and implementing their career plan (Severy, 2011). Reporting most often in student affairs, this organizational structure offers the opportunity for career services departments to be part of an overall student development approach from the point the student enters until graduation (Hoff, Kroll, MacKinnon, & Rentz, 2004). To some prospective students, the perception that graduates receive assistance with job placement and secure desirable jobs after graduation can be the tipping point for enrollment decisions (Hossler, 2011).

Career services embodies a developmental approach to help students determine career interests, develop and sharpen skills, acquire practical experience, identify options for graduate education, and prepare for and conduct a job search (Severy, 2011). A wide array of services and programs can be part of a career services department, including interest inventories or assessment tools, assistance with experiential internships, career fairs, online employer databases, career counseling, educational and skill development workshops, an information library about perspective employers or industry, on-campus interviews, and résumé and cover letter review (Severy, 2011). In addition, some campuses may offer assistance with student employment and include alumni access to services. Both centralized and decentralized organizational models are used, although most institutions use a centralized model to reduce duplication of efforts and allow for a more efficient use of fiscal and personnel resources (National Association of Colleges and Employers, 2009, as cited in Severy, 2011). A decentralized model, where career services departments are located in specific academic colleges, provides a more direct link to the academic programs and faculty and the ability to customize services (Severy, 2011). Opportunities for faculty collaboration include designing résumés or academic-program-specific materials, attending networking events, requesting alumni to update their contact information, having a representative from the office speak during a class session, and encouraging students to attend events sponsored by career services.

Housing and residential life (housing operations, residential programs and policies, facilities, dining services). Residence halls on college campuses have transformed from places where students eat and sleep to places where they grow, develop, and learn (Akens & Novak, 2011). Although largely considered a four-year college campus operation, some community colleges have had residential facilities for decades to attract and retain students, offer affordable housing, and eliminate geographic barriers to educational access (Moeck, Hardy, & Katsinas, 2007). Offering programs and managing the physical environment is the two-pronged mission of housing and residence life departments (Schuh, 2004, as cited in Akens & Novak,

2011). As the first part of its two-part mission, housing and residence life departments create and enforce policies and hall management regulations that foster a student's autonomy and integrity, encourage the development of a community within the halls, balance a student's desire for privacy with the need for interaction, and incorporate academic programming into the halls (Akens & Novak, 2011).

Living–learning communities (LLC) are the most concrete way to integrate academic goals within the residential experience (Zeller, 2006). These programs enable students to take several courses together and live in the same residential building or floor, thus offering integrated learning where the residential community serves as a connection between curricular and cocurricular learning. Whether an LLC is focused on a common topic of interest (e.g., global warming, Going GREEN), an academic major (e.g., engineering, foreign languages), or a lifestyle (e.g., substance free, wellness), students are responsible to each other in the learning process, a key contributor to retention (Tinto, 2003). Students in LLCs reported growth in critical thinking skills and knowledge application, greater interaction with peers and faculty, academic and social integration, commitment to civic engagement, an academically and socially supportive environment, and positive faculty relationships (Inkelas, Szelényi, Soldner, & Brower, 2007).

The second part of the mission, managing the environment, involves the operations aspect of the residence halls, including maintenance needs and repairs, negotiation of dining contracts, housing assignments and room selection processes, budget preparation, technology, safety and security, and the oversight of summer camps and conferences (Akens & Novak, 2011). At some institutions, responsibility for some or all of the operations aspects of facility management may report to other divisions such as in business affairs with other operations-oriented units.

Multicultural student services (multicultural programs and centers; lesbian, gay, bisexual, transgender, and queer [LGBTQ] services and programs; women student services; adult student services; international student services and programs; disability support services; veterans' services). Multicultural student services, initially called minority student services, originated in the 1960s on campuses and focused on offering support and services to single identity groups (Shuford, 2011). The increasing diversity and presence of underrepresented groups (e.g., LGBTQ, women, adults, international students, students with disabilities, and religious diversity) broadened the scope of the focus to include group differences and individual identity groups. Thus, multicultural student services emerged to offer students who experience marginalization or isolation physical space, activities, programs, and educational efforts (targeted toward both majority and underrepresented students) that affirm their culture and assist them in resolving the inconsistencies with their experiences (Shuford, 2011).

Collaborative opportunities with faculty and academic colleges are plentiful through cosponsoring programs, attending programs, integrating programmatic offerings into the curriculum, encouraging student participation, consulting with professional staff on student and campus issues, joining committees that address the needs of multicultural students, advising multicultural student clubs or organizations, and participating in ally programs.

Student conduct (judicial programs, conflict management services). Student discipline has evolved over time from a control and punitive perspective to a more educative and developmental one (Lowery, 2011). The latter perspective situates the student–institutional relationship as educational, which focuses institutional response on behavior that affects the pursuit of the mission (Lowery, 2011). This approach places the mission of the institution at the forefront; maintaining order and an atmosphere conducive to learning is essential (Lowery, 2011). Thus, the primary goal is to develop behavioral standards and expectations for students and address violations of those standards. Students are challenged to take responsibility for their behavior, evaluate the impact their behavior has had on the community (residential, campus, or surrounding), and identify choices they can make to prevent this situation from occurring again. Depending on the mission of the office and institution, students on many campuses are now accountable for behavior exhibited on or off campus, as the courts have sided with institutional authority to regulate off-campus behavior when it affects the institutional mission (Lowery, 2011).

The process of adjudicating student misconduct is often a precise one. Public institutions are mandated legally to provide due process to students, including an articulated series of procedures. Alternatively, because private institutions are not engaged in state action and have a contractual relationship with students, they have more autonomy and are not necessarily required to afford students procedural due process (Lowery, 2011). Larger institutions may have a more decentralized, legalistic, and formal approach when adjudicating students, whereas smaller and private institutions might have a centralized and informal approach (Lowery, 2011). Institutions with large (or exclusively) commuter populations tend to have considerably fewer disciplinary cases than campuses with significant numbers of traditional-age students who reside on or near campus.

In addition to workload, the process to adjudicate cases may differ. Campuses may use one or more methods, including an individual meeting with the conduct officer or a hearing with the campus conduct board composed of students and faculty or staff who receive specialized training. A wide range of sanctions is available to professional staff that can be characterized as punitive (written or oral warnings, disciplinary probation, revocation of privileges, monetary compensation, suspension, or dismissal) and educational (counseling, medical referrals, community service, or projects designed to enhance awareness) (Lowery, 2011). In formal processes, faculty involvement often takes the form of conduct board participation, policy and procedural review processes, conflict resolution and mediation, and referrals for misconduct in the classroom.

Student health services (primary medical care services, health education and prevention, mental health and counseling services). Student health services extend beyond the treatment of illness and are far more comprehensive than ever before. The population they serve and the availability of health care resources in the communities in which they are located influence these programs (Keeling, Avery, Dickson, & Whipple, 2011). Therefore, the range of services differs significantly across institutional types. For example, urban and commuter institutions and community colleges often offer limited services, as students rely on community resources for health care (Keeling et al., 2011). In addition, the inclusion of counseling center services under the umbrella of health services is not uniform across college campuses (American College Health Association, 2010).

Primary medical care services are basic services designed to address minor illness and injury and routine preventative care (women's and men's care, immunizations, chronic illness, infection screening, and laboratory and dispensary services) (Keeling et al., 2011). Health promotions and wellness initiatives provide programming and services that educate students about the impact of their decisions or behaviors on learning and their health and well-being (Keeling et al., 2011). Peer educators, students with extensive training, are often used for much of the educational programming and outreach.

The goal of mental health and counseling services is to help students navigate the key developmental tasks (social and emotional) (Chickering & Reisser, 1993) and cope with various relationship issues (family, significant other) and the stress commonly associated with college attendance. Counseling centers may offer a range of services, such as individual and group counseling; crisis intervention and emergency services; outreach programming; consultation services with other campus constituents (including faculty); training for faculty, staff, peer mentors, and resident assistants; availability of self-help materials (books, audio); and referral services (Zhang, Brandel, & McCoy, 2011). The student demand for counseling services on many campuses has risen significantly in the past two decades (Gallagher, 2013; Kadison & DiGeronimo, 2004; Rando, Barr, & Aros, 2008), prompting evaluation and diversification of services (Zhang et al., 2011). Because campus counseling services are not typically designed for long-term care, many centers limit the number of visits and make referrals to appropriate community agencies or group programs (Zhang et al., 2011).

Although attending to the health needs of students is a major focus, campus health care professionals should play a significant role in policy development and interpretation, such as immunization requirements, alcohol and other drug abuse, suicide prevention, and sexual harassment and assault (Keeling et al., 2011), as well as educating campus constituencies about legal obligations. In addition to the protections afforded to students under the Family Educational Rights and Privacy Act (1974) student health services is governed by the Health Insurance Portability and Accountability Act (HIPAA), which protects patients' records and information from disclosure, including to parents, without the permission of the student (Keeling et al., 2011).

ADDITIONAL EXPERTISE AND RESPONSIBILITIES

In addition to all of the responsibilities and expertise that student affairs professionals have in their individual departments, the division of student affairs and its professionals are primarily involved with or offer significant support to two important elements on college campuses: crisis management and an increased emphasis on Title IX (1972).

Crisis Management

The president as senior executive officer of the institution has a central role in a campus crisis. However, the involvement of other senior-level administrators is likely on many campuses. The student affairs division and its professional staff may provide leadership and typically are the first responders in a crisis, particularly if there is a residential population. The vice president of student affairs, the dean of students, or an appropriate designee may serve as the coordinating entity working with constituencies (i.e., campus police, the president, counseling services, health services, provost, chaplain, residence life, community emergency responders, and local and state police). Significant events such as the death of a student or students and the subsequent impact on the campus community, weather emergencies (e.g., flood, hurricane, tornado), criminal acts and violence, and health conditions or outbreaks (e.g., severe acute respiratory syndrome [SARS], meningitis) are examples of events that many communities, including college campuses, have experienced.

To deal effectively with these types of situations, many campuses have existing crisis management teams led by the provost, vice president for administration, or vice president for student affairs, depending on the institution and the nature of the crisis. In the event of a student death, the student affairs division may be integral to notifying the family, hosting the family members as they retrieve the student's belongings from campus, and coordinating counseling and mental health support programs to help the campus community (students, faculty, and staff) affected by the death.

Large-scale examples of crises affecting college campuses include Hurricane Katrina; the Texas A&M University bonfire tragedy; the California State University, Northridge earthquake; the University of Florida serial killer; and the Virginia Tech shootings. All of these types of crises affect the campus community in varying ways and may involve a cross section of campus leadership; however, student affairs professionals are critical as the crisis unfolds, in the midst of the crisis, and in the aftermath of coping with and moving on from tragedy and loss.

Title IX

Enacted in 1972, Title IX (1972) provided for a number of opportunities for women in education and is best known for addressing equity for women particularly related to participation in athletics and other activities at the high school and college levels. The implications requiring educational institutions receiving federal financial assistance (e.g., student financial aid, research grants) to ensure protection of students, faculty, and staff against sexual harassment and sexual violence (Buzuvis, 2013) have been relatively unnoticed and disregarded.. Renewed scrutiny by the federal government regarding sexual violence resulted in the Dear Colleague Letter (U.S. Department of Education, Office for Civil Rights, 2011), which outlined the requirements and obligations institutions have and defined *sexual harassment* and *sexual violence*.

Student affairs professionals on college campuses have a prominent role in addressing student conduct and behavioral issues; consequently, student-to-student sexual harassment or violence falls directly within their purview. Title IX (1972) does not limit sexual harassment and sexual violence incidences solely to students; it addresses behavior of this nature by and between faculty, administrators, and staff. Student affairs professionals' expertise and experience lies in addressing, resolving, or adjudicating the charges of sexual harassment or sexual violence and providing appropriate assistance and support to the student victims. In addition, they have responsibilities in helping to ensure that the institution is complying with Title IX. Violations of this legislation have extensive implications for campuses that reach far beyond the scope of student affairs, and thus their role may vary based on the incident, the accused, and the campus culture and may take the form of support and consultation with other campus leadership.

CONCLUSION

The development of student affairs on college campuses is attributed to a concern for discipline, housing, counseling, changing student populations, the land-grant movement, curricular reform, the proliferation of the cocurriculum, and expanding enrollments (Williamson, 1961). The evolution of student personnel workers to student affairs professionals resulted from the dramatic transformation in faculty roles and responsibilities, the changes in the institutional relationship with students, the adoption of student development theory as a foundational philosophy, and the formalization of graduate education as an important and essential element of professional preparation for student affairs administrators.

Understanding the roles, responsibilities, and departmental mission and goals of student affairs can serve to transcend the traditional boundaries in the academy to enhance the educational experience for students. Students cross these so-called boundaries every day, and they experience learning in multiple venues and formats. Collaborative efforts between academic affairs and student affairs that connect learning in a seamless fashion will shape the nature of learning, focus the campus environment, and potentially provide evidence of the value added and learning outcomes of college attendance in a more comprehensive manner.

REFERENCES

Akens, C., & Novak, J. (2011). Residence halls. In N. Zhang (Ed.), *Rentz's student affairs practice in higher education* (pp. 315–358). Springfield, IL: Charles C. Thomas.

American Association for Higher Education, American College Personnel Association, & National Association of Student Personnel Administrators. (1998). *Powerful partnerships: A shared responsibility for learning.* Washington, DC: American College Personnel Association.

American College Health Association. (2010). Considerations for integration of counseling and health services on college and university campuses. *Journal of American College Health, 58*(6), 583–596.

American College Personnel Association. (1994). *The student learning imperative: Implications for student affairs.* Washington, DC: Author. Retrieved from www.myacpa .org/sites/default/files/ACPA's%20Student%20Learning%20Imperative.pdf

American College Personnel Association & National Association of Student Personnel Administrators. (1998). *Principles of good practice for student affairs.* Washington, DC: Author.

American Council on Education. (1937). *The student personnel point of view.* Washington, DC: Author. Retrieved from www.myacpa.org/sites/default/files/ student-personnel-point-of-view-1937.pdf

American Council on Education. (1949). *The student personnel point of view.* Washington, DC: Author. Retrieved from www.myacpa.org/sites/default/files/ student-personnel-point-of-view-1949.pdf

Bogue, E. G., & Aper, J. (2000). *Exploring the heritage of American higher education: The evolution of philosophy and policy.* Phoenix, AZ: American Council on Education and Oryx Press.

Brown, R. D. (1972). *Student development in tomorrow's higher education: A return to the academy.* Alexandria, VA: American College Personnel Association.

Brown, T. (2008). Critical concepts in advisor training and development. In V. N. Gordon, W. S. Habley, & T. J. Grites (Eds.), *Academic advising: A comprehensive handbook* (2nd ed., pp. 309–322). San Francisco, CA: Jossey-Bass.

Brubacher, J., & Rudy, W. (2004). *Higher education in transition: A history of American higher colleges and universities, 1636–1976* (4th ed.). New York, NY: Harper and Row.

Buzuvis, E. E. (2013). Introduction: The fortieth anniversary of Title IX. *Western New England Law Review, 35,* 319–321.

Campbell, S. M. (2008). Vision, mission, goals, and program objectives for academic advising programs. In V. N. Gordon, W. S. Habley, & T. J. Grites (Eds.),

Academic advising: A comprehensive handbook (2nd ed., pp. 229–241). San Francisco, CA: Jossey-Bass.

Chickering, A. W., & Reisser, L. R. (1993). *Education and identity* (2nd ed.). San Francisco, CA: Jossey-Bass.

Colwell, B. W. (2006). Partners in a community of learners: Student and academic affairs at small colleges. In S. B. Westfall (Ed.), *The small college dean: New directions for student services, No. 116* (pp. 53–66). San Francisco, CA: Jossey-Bass.

Coomes, M. D., & Talbot, D. M. (2000). *Directory of graduate programs in college student personnel, 1999.* Washington, DC: American College Personnel Association.

Council for Opportunity in Education. (2016). What is TRIO? Retrieved from www.coenet.us/coe_prod_imis/COE/TRIO/History/COE/NAV_TRIO/TRIO_History.aspx?hkey=89b3a80a-3a9e-4580-9fda-38156b9318f8

Cowley, W. H. (1937). A preface to the principles of student counseling. *Educational Record, 18,* 217.

Dale, P. A., & Drake, T. M. (2005). Connecting academic and student affairs to enhance student learning and success. In S. R. Helfgot & M. M. Culp (Eds.), *Community college student affairs: What really matters? New directions for community colleges, No. 131* (pp. 51–64). San Francisco, CA: Jossey-Bass.

DeSawal, D. M., Hornak, A. M., & Mueller, J. A. (Eds.). (2011). *Directory of graduate programs preparing student affairs professionals.* Retrieved from http://gradprograms.myacpa.org

Dungy, G., & Gordon, S. A. (2011). The development of student affairs. In J. H. Schuh, S. R. Jones, & S. R. Harper (Eds.), *Student services: A handbook for the profession* (5th ed., pp. 61–79). San Francisco, CA: Jossey-Bass.

Emmet, T. A., & Sheldon, M. A. (1965). COSPA proposal for college student personnel professional preparation. *NASPA Journal, 3*(1), 45–47.

Family Educational Rights and Privacy Act, 20 U.S.C. § 1232g, 34 CFR Part 99 (1974).

Gallagher, R. (2013). *National survey of counseling center directors* (Monograph Series No. 9U). Alexandria, VA: International Association of Counseling Services. Retrieved from www.collegecounseling.org/wp-content/uploads/Final_Clinicians_v04.pdf

Gaston-Gayles, J. L., Wolf-Wendel, L. E., Tuttle, K. N., Twombly, S. B., & Ward, K. (2005). From disciplinarian to change agent: How the civil rights era changed the roles of student affairs professionals. *NASPA, 42*(3), 263–282.

Gerda, J. J. (2004). *A history of the conferences of deans of women, 1903–1922* (Doctoral dissertation). Bowling Green State University, Ohio. Retrieved from http://search.proquest.com/pqdtft/docview/305217132/fulltextPDF/1319F60 C45E2B7BFA2D/1?accountid=11652

Haynes, R. M., & Bush, V. B. (2011). Student financial aid practice. In N. Zhang (Ed.), *Rentz's student affairs practice in higher education* (pp. 396–426). Springfield, IL: Charles C. Thomas.

Hirt, J. B. (2006). *Where you work matters: Student affairs administration at different types of institutions.* Lanham, MD: University Press of America.

Hirt, J. B. (2007). The student affairs profession in the academic marketplace. *NASPA Journal, 44*(2), 245–264.

Hoff, K. S., Kroll, J., MacKinnon, F. J. D., & Rentz, A. L. (2004). Career services. In F. J. D. MacKinnon (Ed.), *Rentz's student affairs practice in higher education* (pp. 108–143). Springfield, IL: Charles C. Thomas.

Hossler, D. (2000). The role of financial aid in enrollment management. In M. D. Coomes (Ed.), *The role student aid plays in enrollment management: New directions for student services, No. 89* (pp. 77–90). San Francisco, CA: Jossey-Bass.

Hossler, D. (2011). From admission to enrollment management. In N. Zhang (Ed.), *Rentz's student affairs practice in higher education* (pp. 63–95). Springfield, IL: Charles C. Thomas.

Inkelas, K. K., Szelényi, K., Soldner, M., & Brower, A. M. (2007). *The national study of living-learning programs: 2007 report of findings.* College Park, MD: Author. Retrieved from http://drum.lib.umd.edu/bitstream/handle/1903/8392/2007%20 NSLLP%20Final%20Report.pdf?sequence=1&isAllowed=y

Kadison, R., & DiGeronimo, T. F. (2004). *College of the overwhelmed: The campus mental health crisis and what to do about it.* San Francisco, CA: Jossey-Bass.

Keeling, R. P. (Ed.). (2004). *Learning reconsidered: A campus-wide focus on the student experience.* Washington, DC: American College Personnel Association & National Association of Student Personnel Administrators.

Keeling, R. P. (Ed.). (2006). *Learning reconsidered 2: A practical guide to implementing a campus-wide focus on the student experience.* Washington, DC: American College Personnel Association, Association of College and University Housing Officers-International, Association of College Unions International, National Association of Campus Activities, National Academic Advising Association, National Association of Student Personnel Administrators, & National Intramural-Recreational Sports Association.

Keeling, R. P., Avery, T., Dickson, J. S. M., & Whipple, E. G. (2011). Student health. In N. Zhang (Ed.), *Rentz's student affairs practice in higher education* (pp. 430–459). Springfield, IL: Charles C. Thomas.

Kezar, A. (2009). Supporting and enhancing student learning through partnerships with academic colleagues. In G. S. McClellan & J. Stringer (Eds.), *The hand-*

book of student affairs administration (3rd ed., pp. 405–424). San Francisco, CA: Jossey-Bass.

King, M. (2008). Organization of academic advising services. In V. N. Gordon, W. S. Habley, & T. J. Grites (Eds.), *Academic advising: A comprehensive handbook* (2nd ed., pp. 242–252). San Francisco, CA: Jossey-Bass.

Kuh, G. D. (1996). Guiding principles for creating seamless learning environments for undergraduates. *Journal of College Student Development, 37*, 135–148.

Kuh, G. D., & Hinkle, S. A. (2002). Enhancing student learning through collaboration between academic affairs and student affairs. In R. M. Diamond (Ed.), *Field guide to academic leadership* (pp. 311–327). San Francisco, CA: Jossey-Bass.

Kuh, G. D., Schuh, J. H., Whitt, E. J., & Associates. (1991). *Involving colleges: Successful approaches to fostering student learning and development outside the classroom.* San Francisco, CA: Jossey-Bass.

Love, P. G., Kuh, G. D., MacKay, K. A., & Hardy, C. M. (1993). Side by side: Faculty and student affairs cultures. In G. D. Kuh (Ed.), *Cultural perspectives in student affairs work* (pp. 37–58). Lanham, MD: American College Personnel Association.

Lowery, J. W. (2011). Student conduct. In N. Zhang (Ed.), *Rentz's student affairs practice in higher education* (pp. 196–244). Springfield, IL: Charles C. Thomas.

Manning, K., Kinzie, J., & Schuh, J. (2006). *One size does not fit all: Traditional and innovative models of student affairs practice.* New York, NY: Routledge.

McEwen, M. K. (2003). The nature and use of theory. In S. R. Komives & D. B. Woodard, Jr., (Eds.), *Student services: A handbook for the profession* (4th ed., pp. 153–178). San Francisco, CA: Jossey-Bass.

Moeck, P. G., Hardy, D. E., & Katsinas, S. G. (2007). Residential living at rural community colleges. In P. M. Eddy & J. P. Murray (Eds.), *Rural community colleges: Teaching, learning and leading in the heartland: New directions for community colleges, No. 137* (pp. 77–86). San Francisco, CA: Jossey-Bass.

Overland, W. I., Rentz, A. L., & Sarnicki, M. L. (2011). Orientation. In N. Zhang (Ed.), *Rentz's student affairs practice in higher education* (pp. 281–314). Springfield, IL: Charles C. Thomas.

Pascarella, E. T., & Terenzini, P. (2005). *How college affects students: A third decade of research* (Vol. 2). San Francisco, CA: Jossey-Bass.

Rando, R., Barr, V., & Aros, C. (2008). The Association for University and College Counseling Center 2007 directors annual survey. Retrieved from http://files.cmcglobal.com/aucccd_monograph_public_2008.pdf

Rentz, A. L., & Howard-Hamilton, M. (2011). Student affairs: An historical perspective. In N. Zhang (Ed.), *Rentz's student affairs practice in higher education* (4th ed., pp. 30–62). Springfield, IL: Charles C. Thomas.

Rhatigan, J. J. (2009). From the people up: A brief history of student affairs administration. In G. S. McClellan & J. Stringer (Eds.), *The handbook of student affairs administration* (3rd ed., pp. 3–18). San Francisco, CA: Jossey-Bass.

Rudolph, F. (1990). *The American college and university: A history.* Athens, GA: University of Georgia.

Sandeen, A. (2001). Organizing student affairs divisions. In R. B. Winston, Jr., D. G. Creamer, & T. K. Miller (Eds.), *The professional student affairs administrator* (pp. 181–210). New York, NY: Brunner-Routledge.

Schuster, J. H., & Finkelstein, M. J. (2011). The American faculty in perspective. In S. R. Harper & J. F. L. Jackson (Eds.), *Introduction to American higher education* (pp. 5–18). New York, NY: Routledge.

Schwartz, R. A. (2002). The rise and demise of deans of men. *The Review of Higher Education, 26*(2), 217–239. Retrieved from https://muse.jhu.edu/article/45170/pdf

Severy, L. (2011). Career services. In N. Zhang (Ed.), *Rentz's student affairs practice in higher education* (pp. 119–150). Springfield, IL: Charles C. Thomas.

Shuford, B. C. (2011). Multicultural affairs. In N. Zhang (Ed.), *Rentz's student affairs practice in higher education* (pp. 245–280). Springfield, IL: Charles C. Thomas.

Study Group on the Conditions of Excellence in American Higher Education. (1984). *Involvement in learning: Realizing the potential of American higher education.* Washington, DC: National Institution of Education.

Thelin, J. R. (2004). *A history of American higher education.* Baltimore, MD: Johns Hopkins University Press.

Tinto, V. (2003). *Learning better together: The impact of learning communities on student success* (Higher Education Monograph Series, No. 1). Syracuse, NY: School of Education, Syracuse University. Retrieved August 15, 2011, from www.nhcuc.org/pdfs/Learning_Better_Together.pdf

Title IX 20 U.S.C. §§ 1682 *et seq.*, 34 C.F.R. Part 106 (1972).

U.S. Department of Education, Office for Civil Rights. (2011). *Dear colleague letter: Sexual violence background, summary and fast facts.* Washington, DC: Author. Retrieved from www2.ed.gov/about/offices/list/ocr/letters/colleague-201104.pdf

Whipple, E. G., & O'Neill, K. B. (2011). Student activities. In N. Zhang (Ed.), *Rentz's student affairs practice in higher education* (pp. 359–395). Springfield, IL: Charles C. Thomas.

Williamson, E. G. (1961). *Student personnel services in colleges and universities.* New York, NY: McGraw-Hill.

Wrenn, C. G. (1959). Philosophical and psychological bases of personnel services in education. In *Personnel services in education, 58th yearbook of the National Society of the Study of Education, Part II* (p. 47). Chicago, IL: University of Chicago.

Zeller, W. J. (2006). Academic integration and campus transformation. In B. M. McCluskey & N. W. Dunkel (Eds.), *Foundations: Strategies for the future of collegiate housing* (pp. 59–66). Columbus, OH: Association of College and University Housing Officers International.

Zhang, N., Brandel, I. W., & McCoy, V. A. (2011). Counseling centers. In N. Zhang (Ed.), *Rentz's student affairs practice in higher education* (pp. 151–195). Springfield, IL: Charles C. Thomas.

2

Student Development Theory in Academic Affairs

Ellen M. Broido

MANY FACTORS INFLUENCE THE design of policies and practices regarding work with undergraduate students. We do things because they are cost-effective, because they are politically expedient, and because they are in the best interests of the university. In a perfect world, the only considerations in the design of programs and policies would be that they promote the development and success of students; encourage students' movement toward graduation and academic achievement; and enhance students' critical thinking skills, ability to be effective and engaged citizens, understanding of themselves and others, interest in lifelong learning, and ability and decision to act ethically (Association of American Colleges and Universities, 2007). Although few, if any, of us, work in such perfect universities where these are the only priorities, understanding how students grow while in college and what supports their development of these outcomes provides an optimal place from which to make decisions about policies and programs.

Models of student development describe "the evolution of *skills* ([emphasis added] defined broadly to include abilities, capacities, ways of understanding) over time, where early level skills are reorganized into higher-level skills that allow individuals to manage more complex units of information, perspectives, and tasks" (King, 2009, p. 598). In relation to college students, developmental models most commonly are split into psychosocial models and cognitive-structural

37

models, both outgrowths of psychology and, to a lesser extent, sociology. These fields proposed models of human development across the lifespan.

With the increasing turbulence of college campuses in the 1960s came attempts to understand the developmental changes experienced specifically by college students. This in turn gave rise to early models of student development, in particular Chickering's (1969) model of psychosocial development and Perry's (1970) model of cognitive development. More recent findings suggest that psychosocial and cognitive development are more interdependent than previously hypothesized, giving rise to integrative models of development. These three clusters of developmental models (psychosocial, cognitive, and integrative), along with their application to academic affairs, are the focus of this chapter.

PSYCHOSOCIAL MODELS OF DEVELOPMENT

Psychosocial models of development address "how [*students*] [emphasis added] define themselves, how they relate to others, and what they choose to do with their lives" (Hamrick, Evans, & Schuh, 2002, p. 34). According to this group of theories, "at various points throughout the life course, different concerns will take precedence and become major challenges the individual must resolve in order to advance" (Hamrick et al., 2002, p. 33). This group of models is derived from the work of Erik Erikson (1959, 1968), who studied development from infancy through old age. Erikson proposed that in young adulthood, people are typically concerned with identity and intimate relationships. Those studying the development of college students more closely examined these two stages, giving rise to several models that explain various aspects of identity and intimacy development.

Chickering and Reisser

In 1969, Arthur Chickering wrote what many consider to be the foundational text on student development theory, *Education and Identity*. Chickering and Linda Reisser revised this book in 1993 to be more inclusive of the range of students then enrolling in higher education. The revised model identifies seven primary domains (also termed *vectors*) in which students change during college: *developing* (intellectual, physical/manual, and interpersonal) *competence, managing emotions, moving through autonomy toward interdependence, developing mature interpersonal relationships, establishing identity, developing purpose*, and *developing integrity*.

Although students' energy tends to focus on only a few vectors at a time, the vectors are addressed somewhat sequentially. Entering students tend to be concerned with developing competence and managing emotions, and concerns regarding purpose and integrity are foci toward the ends of students' careers. Vectors are never fully mastered or completed; most entering graduate students will attest to concerns about intellectual competence and fighting battles anew in managing their emotions.

Although helping students develop a sense of identity is not normally considered within the scope of academic affairs, data indicate measures of a sense of identity correlate with students' grade point average at approximately 0.30, and an even higher correlation is noted for African American students (Lounsbury, Huffstetler, Leong, & Gibson, 2005). The development of intellectual competence bears obvious relationship to academic success, but the other vectors are important as well. Students unable to manage their emotions have limited ability to cope with the frustrations of challenging material, performance not at their usual level, the anxiety of exams, or the self-discipline to prioritize studying over more enjoyable pursuits. Students either are overly dependent on their peers' approval or are fiercely independent, poor members of group projects and teams, and likely to reject the efforts of authority figures trying to be helpful.

Marcia and Josselson

Another cluster of models of psychosocial development was developed by James Marcia (1966) and Ruthellen Josselson (1987, 1996). Marcia's original work focused only on men, and Josselson adapted his basic framework to understand the development of women. In both models, Erikson's (1959, 1968) concept of identity crisis is foundational; Erikson believed this to be the primary concern of young adults. In both Marcia's and Josselson's models, students are categorized depending on (a) whether they have experienced a crisis or explored their values and (b) whether they have made a commitment to a foundational set of values, yielding four groups (also termed *statuses*): *foreclosure* (no crisis, committed to values with which they were raised), *moratorium* (crisis, no commitment), *diffusion* (no crisis, no commitment), and *identity achievement* (crisis of values, considered commitment to current values). Optimally, students will reach identity achievement, but "healthy and unhealthy choices exist within each status" (Evans, Forney, Guido, Patton, & Renn, 2010, p. 53). Marcia found that men typically experience crises around political, religious, and occupational choices, whereas Josselson found that women's crises tended to focus more on religious or sexual values and what kind of people they wanted to be.

These theories tell us that it is normal for students to be questioning major values and decisions in their lives and suggest that academic affairs administrators help students critically consider choices that seem to have been made without consideration of other possibilities. It is not wrong for students to adopt values of their families or peers, but if they have done so without careful consideration, it is likely they will be revisited later on when changes become more difficult. Similarly, these models encourage us to be patient while students struggle to define their values and relationships and remind us that these decisions take time, and uncertainty is developmentally appropriate. We should avoid pushing students to make major decisions too soon.

COGNITIVE MODELS OF DEVELOPMENT

Derived from the work of Jean Piaget (1952), models of cognitive development trace changes in how students understand what is truth or knowledge, what role evidence and authorities play in their understanding of "right" answers, and how they decide what is moral. In contrast with psychosocial models, which focus on the content of students' thinking, cognitive models focus on students' thought processes.

Epistemological and Cognitive-Structural Models

The foundational cognitive development model relating to college students was that of William Perry (1970), who studied the development of Harvard (and a very few Radcliffe) students in the early 1960s, replicated in the early 1970s and 1980s (Evans et al., 2010). Although a number of theorists have expanded on Perry's theory, the language he used to label the series of positions in his model remains the most commonly used parlance. Perry proposed nine positions, several of which have multiple forms, and he also identified transitional positions. Although Perry provided a great deal of detail about the earlier positions, the final three positions of his model were less well developed, and later theorists have not further explicated them (Love & Guthrie, 1999). The explanation is focused on the earlier stages and combines them into three groups, as they are most commonly used in practical application.

Perry and his team found that most students began college reasoning in a way they termed *dualism*, in which authority figures have the right answers, all questions have a single right or best answer, and the role of the student is to memorize the right answer given by authorities. It is the right–wrong, good–bad polarization that gives this position its name.

Growth happens when students encounter authorities who disagree, who refuse to identify a single right answer, who state that right answers are not yet known, or who indicate there might not be a "right" answer. This cognitive dissonance forces students to reevaluate their beliefs about how one knows anything and who can be trusted, and it moves them into the next position, *multiplicity*. In this position, students come to believe that there are no standards for evaluating knowledge or truth and that each person's perspective is as valid as any other. In multiplicity, peers' views are to be respected (although not necessarily agreed with), and students see their role as understanding the thinking processes of their faculty, rather than receiving and memorizing facts (Cornfield & Knefelkamp, 1979, as cited in Knefelkamp, 1970/1999).

Some students (but not all) (Love & Guthrie, 1999) begin to recognize that not all arguments are equally valid, in part because their faculty and other authority figures require them to evaluate arguments and justify their conclusions. What students start doing as an academic exercise to please authorities becomes recognized as a legitimate way of understanding the relative and context-bound nature of knowledge and truth. Students gradually come to recognize that evidence and data make some positions or conclusions more reasonable, plausible, or likely than others. In this position of *relativism*, students see answers to complex issues as provisional rather than absolute, and students realize that data and evidence may expand and change, leading to new conclusions. In addition, reasonable people may interpret evidence differently and thus logically come to different conclusions. All authorities' "assertions are now open to analysis, evaluation, and the requirements of contextualized evidence" (Love & Guthrie, 1999, p. 12).

Perry found students' growth was not necessarily linear, and some students spent longer in one position than did their peers or, under periods of stress, regressed to dualism. Perry also described additional stages of growth that did not reflect changes in cognitive structures and thus are not addressed here.

Many theorists have built on Perry's work. Those most commonly referenced in describing student development are the work of Belenky, Clinchy, Goldberger, and Tarule (1986), who described changes in women's cognitive development, looking both at women college graduates and at women receiving social services; Baxter Magolda (1992, 1998, 2001), whose work will be discussed later in this chapter; and King and Kitchener (1994; Kitchener & King, 1981, 1990).

King and Kitchener (1994) studied both women's and men's development of reflective judgment as

> the developmental progression that occurs between childhood and adulthood in the ways that people understand the process of knowing and in the corresponding ways that they justify their beliefs about ill-structured problems. . . . As individuals develop, they become better able to evaluate knowledge claims and to explain and defend their points of view on controversial issues. (p. 13)

King and Kitchener (1994) were concerned with the epistemic assumptions people use in solving what they called *ill-structured problems*, complex issues that "cannot be described with a high degree of completeness or solved with a high degree of certainty" (p. 10). Through this they developed a seven-stage model broken into three phases. In *pre-reflective* thinking, knowledge is certain (or temporarily uncertain), and authorities have or will learn the answer. In *quasi-reflective* thinking, answers to ill-structured problems are recognized as uncertain but are resolved more as a matter of personal belief than evaluation of evidence. People in this stage do not yet think it is possible to evaluate evidence and knowledge claims and thus rely on personal preference or avoid coming to conclusions. Finally, in *reflective* thinking, people come to recognize that some sources and claims are better supported than others, and knowledge claims are understood to reflect the preponderance of credible evidence and authorities and are subject to revision in light of new data (King & Kitchener, 1994).

There are several caveats to King and Kitchener's (1994) findings that have important implications for the design of policies and procedures. The first is that students typically function within a range of stages, with an optimal level used when students are confident, working with familiar subject matter, and not facing stressors. More typical, students process and function from an earlier level of reasoning, especially when dealing with new subject matter or when tired, threatened, or stressed.

Second, on average, students enter college reasoning roughly between the third and fourth stages (on the cusp between pre-reflective and quasi-reflective thinking) and leave reasoning solidly within the fourth stage (quasi-reflective thinking). Although one half a stage of growth may seem very small, it represents a critical qualitative change from "ignorant certainty" to "intelligent confusion" (Kroll, 1992, as cited in Love & Guthrie, 1999, p. 50). This represents a radically different way of understanding the nature of knowledge, argument, and truth and, although perhaps still short of what we desire of college graduates (Association of American Colleges and Universities, 2007), is nevertheless profound growth. King and Kitchener (1994) saw the entry into quasi-reflective thinking, typically only in the senior year, as the most significant developmental advance, noting that this is the first significant "acknowledgment of the uncertainty of knowledge, the ability to differentiate between well- and ill-structured problems, and the ability to work with simple abstract concepts (including 'evidence' and knowledge)" (p. 150). Thus, undergraduate education that presumes facility with the use of evidence to make arguments will not make sense to most students.

King and Kitchener (1994) indicated that situations in which students encounter experiences different from what they expect are powerful stimulators of growth because they require students "to reconsider, reinterpret, or reject prior assumptions or beliefs" that "may lead the person to suspect or realize the drawbacks of prior (or even current) ways of thinking, which leads in turn to the creation of new assumptions and new ways of understanding" (p. 229). In addition, treating all students with respect is critical if they are to take the risk of thinking in new ways. King and Kitchener recommended tailoring interactions with students to their developmental position and specifically encouraging them to use the reasoning strategies of one stage beyond what they are currently using. Another strategy is to introduce students to ill-structured problems in their discipline in introductory courses and to examine these problems from multiple competing perspectives. The instructor role models how to do so and then requires students to judge the adequacy of arguments and provide justification for their conclusions. Finally, providing support for students' current way of reasoning (even when we find it inadequate) is necessary for them to engage in the challenge of thinking in new ways. Although sometimes this support can be structural or cognitive (e.g., using material with which the student is familiar), emotional support is useful as well, particularly because "development in reflective thinking may be disturbing, frustrating, and even frightening to students" (King & Kitchener, 1994, p. 247). For specific strategies to move students between particular stages, see pages 250 through 254 in King and Kitchener's (1994) *Developing Reflective Judgment*.

Moral Development Models

Two models of moral development shape common understandings of student growth in college: Lawrence Kohlberg's (1976, 1984) and Carol Gilligan's (1977, 1982). Models of moral reasoning focus on the process people use to decide what is moral; this process is necessary but not sufficient to determine moral behavior, which also requires (a) recognizing that the situation has a moral component and identifying the moral interests of the relevant parties; (b) prioritizing moral values over other values (e.g., monetary reward, visibility, etc.); and (c) having the "perseverance, ego strength, and implementations skills" to actually behave morally (Rest, 1986, p. 3).

Kohlberg's model traces changes in the reasoning people use to determine what is moral. From a very young age, people make determinations about what is moral or fair, as short scrutiny of any three-year-old's response to a younger sibling taking her ball will demonstrate. Whether and why she thinks it is wrong will (we hope) change over her life, and Kohlberg's model described these changes. As Mayhew and King (2008) noted, Kohlberg described "how the person is approaching the topic, not what specific moral belief or opinion he or she holds" (p. 19).

Drawing from the works of psychologist Jean Piaget and moral philosopher John Rawls, Kohlberg (1976, 1984) described a process of development that included six "invariant and qualitatively different stages" (Evans et al., 2010, p. 101). The first level, known as the *pre-conventional* level, is made up of stages 1 and 2. At this level people's reasoning focuses entirely on themselves and individual others; people at this level are unaware of or uninterested in societal norms and rules. At the first stage, moral behavior is that which does not get one punished; anything unpunished is "good," and authorities have the right to set rules and punish. At the second stage, people are able to distinguish between rules and their own interests and recognize that different people might have different interests, so what is right is determined by what is fair. Equal treatment and fair exchange are critical determinants of what is and is not moral.

In the second level, known as *conventional* reasoning, people's determination of what is moral or fair is shaped by society. "People identify with the rules and expectations of others, especially authorities" (Evans et al., 2010, p. 103), and people strive to be seen, and to think of themselves, as good members of a community. Social approval, conformity, and social stability guide moral decision-making.

In the third level, *post-conventional*, principles replace the views of society as determinants of what is moral, including concepts "such as majority rule, minority rights that are sharable, reciprocal and open to scrutiny by others" (Mayhew & King, 2008, p. 19). Although post-conventional reasoners usually follow social norms and laws, they recognize that the law and morality do not always align, and social norms sometimes must be violated to support universal principles such as "the equality of human rights and respect for the dignity of human beings as individual persons" (Kohlberg, 1976, p. 35).

Kohlberg's model has been updated and expanded on by Rest and colleagues, who developed what is commonly referred to as a neo-Kohlbergian framework. This framework views moral reasoning as likely to span several stages in which "the more primitive ways of thinking are gradually replaced by more complex ways of thinking" (Endicott, Bock, & Narvaez, 2003, p. 406). Thus, although one can speak of the predominant way in which a person reasons, people can understand reasoning more complex than they demonstrate and at times will reason from earlier stages.

Kohlberg argued that growth in moral reasoning required more generalized cognitive development and experience taking others' perspectives (Kohlberg, 1976), along with "exposure to higher-state thinking and disequilibrium" (Evans et al., 2010, p. 102) or cognitive conflict. Although there is convincing evidence that moral reasoning skills correlate strongly with educational level, it is not completely clear what actually causes the development of moral reasoning (Mayhew, Seifert, & Pascarella, 2010). That said, findings from Mayhew and colleagues (2010) indicated specific educational practices can promote development. In particular, "the extent to which students reported that their courses helped them to understand the historical, political, and social connections of past events was positively related to moral reasoning development" (Mayhew et al., 2010, p. 379).

An alternate way of understanding moral reasoning was introduced by Gilligan (1977, 1982), focusing on women's ways of making moral choices. Gilligan's work is one of "correcting and supplementing rather than overturning the Kohlbergian project" (Reed, 1997, p. 221) and shares many key aspects. Gilligan's research found that some people's moral decision-making focused on their responsibility to others and self, with a preeminent value on nonviolence, as contrasted with Kohlberg's focus on fairness and justice. This alternative view is often referred to as *a different voice*, the title of Gilligan's (1982/1993) classic work.

Gilligan (1982) explicitly argued that neither a Kohlbergian *justice* orientation to moral reasoning nor her own description of *care-based* moral decision-making is the sole province of either gender. Later research (e.g., Rest, 1986) has confirmed that both women and men can and do use both kinds of moral decision-making, although care-based decision-making happens more in the context of relationships and real-life dilemmas, and justice-based decision-making happens more often in hypothetical or impersonal situations (Juujärvi, 2005).

In Gilligan's model, moral decision-making moves through three stages, with intermediate transitional stages: *individual survival,* a transition *from selfishness to responsibility*; a middle stage of *self sacrifice and social conformity,* a transition *from goodness to truth*; and a final stage, *morality of nonviolence.*

In individual survival, people focus solely on their own interests; what is right or fair is what meets their own needs and wants. Others' needs and wants either are not recognized or are not as important as one's own survival (Gilligan, 1977). In the transition between the first and second stages, "this judgment is criticized as selfish," reflecting "a new understanding of the connection between self and others which is articulated by the concept of responsibility" (Gilligan, 1982/1993, p. 74). There begins to be recognition that one's own needs are not the only important ones.

In the second stage, self sacrifice and social conformity, "good is equated with caring for others" (Gilligan, 1977, p. 492) and "consensual judgment about goodness becomes the overriding concern as survival is now seen to depend on acceptance by others" (Gilligan, 1982/1993, p. 79). In this stage, conventional feminine values such as caring, self-sacrifice, nurturing, and avoiding hurting others are foundational, overriding the need for individual expression.

In the transition between the second and third stages, a movement described as from goodness to truth, people begin to include themselves in the scope of those who should not be hurt. Gilligan (1982/1993, p. 82) wrote, "The woman begins to ask whether it is selfish or responsible, moral or immoral, to include her own needs within the compass of her care and concern." This perspective requires that people believe in their own "capacity for independent judgment and the legitimacy of [their] own point of view" (Gilligan, 1977, p. 502). The awareness of and valuing of one's own experience, and the consequent validation of one's own needs, begin to supersede the need to be seen as good, and the need to speak and stand for the truth, including one's own truth, becomes predominant as people move into the final stage.

In the final stage of Gilligan's model, the morality of nonviolence, people reach a balance between meeting their own needs and meeting the needs of others, with a focus on responsibility and relationships and a guiding principle of minimizing hurt. There is a rejection of the earlier focus on social approval as the definition of *moral* and an assertion "of moral equality between self and other. Care then becomes a universal obligation" (Gilligan, 1977, p. 504).

Because there is only initial work toward the development of a way of assessing moral decision-making within Gilligan's framework (e.g., Skoe,

1998), little is known about how most college students reason or how much change, if any, is typical over the college years. Research done by Juujärvi (2006) found significant increases in both ethic of care reasoning and ethic of justice reasoning between students' first and third years of undergraduate work among women and men enrolled in nursing and social work programs, but growth only in the ethic of justice reasoning stage in law-enforcement degree seekers. Growth, however, was modest, with only one third of participants showing growth of at least one half stage in care reasoning and not quite one half showing growth of at least one half stage in justice reasoning. Researchers can contribute a great deal in this area.

INTEGRATIVE MODELS

Although cognitive structural and psychosocial models provide a detailed, focused way of understanding change in college students, they are limited by their narrow perspective, disjointing complex human development into artificially distinct processes. Integrative models, in contrast, examine multiple aspects of development simultaneously. Two groups of integrative theories are presented here: models of self-authorship and models addressing social identity development.

Self-Authorship

Although epistemological and psychosocial models held sway for the first 30 years of explicit theories of student development, in the past decade theories of self-authorship have moved to the forefront of research on college student development. These models have a holistic perspective to development, considering interpersonal development, intrapersonal development, and epistemological development simultaneously. In particular, Marcia Baxter Magolda's model of self-authorship (2001, 2008), building on Robert Kegan's (1982, 1994) research, described how college students come to develop (during and through 20 years following their college careers) the fourth of Kegan's five stages of consciousness.

The psychologist Kegan (1982, 1994) described the development of consciousness as "the personal unfolding of ways of organizing experience" (1994, p. 9). He identified five stages (in some writings *order* or *form*) of development, with four intermediate transitions, each an increasingly complex way of understanding what constitutes the self and what constitutes other than oneself, what he referred to as *self* and *object* (Kegan, 1982). Stages describe "the principles by which [people] construct and organize their thinking, feeling, and social relating" (Eriksen, 2007, p. 174) or cognitive, intrapersonal, and interpersonal elements. With each progression in his model, people acquire the ability to examine critically what previously was considered self; the former self (things one is "identified with, tied to, fused with, or embedded in" [Kegan, 1994, p. 32]) is now object, something that can be scrutinized, considered, and reflected on.

Most college students (like most adults) function at the third stage of Kegan's model (Kegan, 1994), in which people gain "the ability to think abstractly, identify a complex internal psychological life, . . . construct values and ideals self-consciously known as such, [and] subordinate one's own interests on behalf of one's greater loyalty to [others]" (Kegan, 1994, p. 77). People in this stage are able to take the perspective of others and to critically examine their own roles as peers, family members, or other social roles (Love & Guthrie, 1999). In this stage, relationships are critical to individuals' conceptions of themselves, and thus they have limited capacity to cope with disruptions to those relationships (Evans et al., 2010) or consider opinions other than those of meaningful others. Kegan argued in his 1994 book *In Over Our Heads* that this way of functioning, although far more effective than that of prior levels, was insufficient to meet "the mental demands of modern life" (the subtitle of his book). To function effectively in a world in which people are expected to provide leadership, manage boundaries, set limits, communicate across difference, and be effective partners and colleagues, people need to move into the fourth order of consciousness in which people gain the capacity to self-author their identities.

Self-authorship, Kegan's fourth stage, involves the ability to determine one's own opinions, ideas, and values—not negating others' perspectives but also not being dictated by them. Relationships no longer are definitional but can be evaluated and modified. As Love and Guthrie (1999) noted, "Students begin to develop an independent selfhood with an ideology of their own. . . . The source of judgment and expectation comes to reside within the self rather than being confused with others" (p. 71). People in this stage have enough perspective on their values to be able to resolve conflicts among them. In short, fourth-order reasoning reflects the kinds of outcomes espoused by many universities for their students: being a "self-directed learner, an individual who acts on the world for the betterment of society (rather than is acted on), and an engaged citizen with a strong sense of values and a clear identity that is internally defined" (p. 73).

Influenced by Kegan's work, Baxter Magolda's research is based on her almost 25-year longitudinal study of changes in students' ways of making meaning. She began following 100 traditionally aged students from their first year in college through graduation and has continued to interview roughly 35 of those participants annually, as they now approach their mid-40s. Although her findings from the undergraduate years focused solely on their epistemological development, as participants entered young adulthood after college, she found that Kegan's (1982, 1994) model better described her participants' growth. In particular, students demonstrated changes in epistemological development, intrapersonal development (understanding "who am I?"), and interpersonal development (relationships with others).

Baxter Magolda's model of self-authorship expanded on existing models of epistemological development in its recognition that

> without an ability to integrate their own internally defined goals, values, and sense of self into their decision-making processes, contextual knowers often make decisions based on logic without considering their own feelings or goals, thus leaving them feeling dissatisfied despite their critical thinking and ability to act autonomously. . . . In addition, self-authorship, as opposed to contextual knowing, allows students to consider their immediate decisions in the context of a large frame of situations, relationships, and goals. (Pizzolato, 2006, p. 33)

Baxter Magolda traced her participants' movement from Kegan's third order to the fourth order as they entered adulthood and identified aspects of the collegiate environment that could facilitate that transition earlier in students' lives. In Baxter Magolda's (2009) terms, this movement was from *external formulas*, moving through a *crossroads*, and culminating in *self-authorship*. Most students start and about 80% leave college using external formulas thinking, in which they "trust authorities to decide what to believe, [and] follow other's visions for how to succeed. External voices (those of others) in the foreground drown out internal voices" (Baxter Magolda, 2009, p. 4). In the crossroads position, students struggle to resolve discrepancies between others' voices and expectations and their own emerging voices and ideas for how they should live their own lives. When students become self-authoring, they "trust [them]selves to decide what to believe, following [their] vision for how to succeed. Internal voice in the foreground coordinates information from external voices" (Baxter Magolda, 2009, p. 4).

Baxter Magolda (2001) noted that environments promoting the development of self-authorship presumed "*that knowledge is complex, ambiguous, and socially constructed in a context,"* that *"an internal sense of self is central to effective participation in the social construction of knowledge,"* and that *"expertise or authority is shared among learners and teachers as they mutually construct knowledge"* (p. 195, italics in original). Baxter Magolda (2001) created the learning partnerships model to explain what approaches fostered this development. These include using practices that ask students to reflect on their current ways of making meaning (i.e., direct questioning, journal prompts, reflective essays) and by providing both support for respecting their own authority and credibility as knowers and a challenge to students' current ways of thinking and relating to others (King & Baxter Magolda, 2011).

In particular, students need support in the form of having their own thoughts, experiences, and perspectives respected by people in authority (thereby teaching them that their own ideas have worth and are due consideration); by having learning based in or starting from their own lived experience (either by being asked to find examples of what they are learning in their own lives or by being asked to practice or otherwise enact what they are learning); and by learning to coconstruct knowledge with authorities rather than passively receiving knowledge (Baxter Magolda, 2001). The challenge entails letting students see that "knowledge is complex and socially constructed," acknowledging that "self is central to knowledge construction," and sharing "authority and expertise" (King & Baxter Magolda, 2011, p. 216) with students.

Social Identity Development

Models of social identity development address how we see ourselves and others as members of groups based on race, gender, religion, sexual orientation, economic status, and other forms of social group identity (Torres, Jones, & Renn, 2009). Understanding of what it means to have these identities often changes while students are in college, especially for groups with relatively less social power (e.g., for women, people of color, non-Christians, those with disabilities, etc.), although it is not uncommon for students to start to critically explore what it means to be members of more privileged groups (e.g., White, male, heterosexual, etc.). Models describing these changes are referred to as social identity development models. Although historically they were considered aspects of psychosocial development, more recently researchers and theorists have recognized that intrapersonal development and epistemological development also profoundly shape how people understand their social identities, and thus they are more often categorized as integrative models (Torres, 2011).

Models exist describing the identity development of African Americans, Latinos, Asian Americans, Native Americans, bi- and multiracial people, European Americans, women, men, lesbians, gay men, heterosexuals, and other social groups. Emerging research is starting to outline the identity development of transgendered people, bisexual people, and social class identity, whereas ability–disability and religious identity still lack widely used models.

Although models describing the development of racial, ethnic, sexual orientation, and gender identities differ in meaningful ways, many identify similar patterns (Burchell & Broido, 1995; Torres et al., 2009). These commonalities include an initial acceptance of dominant perceptions of that identity form's meaning, with privileged identities seen as normal, superior, and natural and members of groups with less social power being "different," lesser, more emotional and less rational, and generally "other." Alternately, or sometimes simultaneously, people in initial stages of identity development may put little salience on that aspect of their identity, choosing to identify with another aspect of themselves. Note that for students who were previously unaware of their identities (e.g., some LBGT students, students who have acquired a disability, students who convert to non-Christian religions, etc.), gaining awareness of their identities would precede this stage.

Movement out of this early stage for students in targeted groups is often prompted by encounters with explicit discrimination or, less often, with members of the group who have passionately positive understandings of their identity. These experiences highlight the importance of the identity to individuals and often cause them to question the stereotypes of their group held by society, redefining those stereotypes in uncritically positive ways. Students in dominant social groups in this stage engage in intense questioning of what they have been taught about their group and the targeted group and withdraw from members of their own group who are not asking similar questions. Typically this stage is marked by high energy and involvement in exploring and redefining this identity, resistance to dominant definitions, and withdrawal from those who maintain negative views about that group. It is not unusual to see students in this stage searching for more accurate and complete information about this issue; engaging in local, national, or international activism; and critically examining and challenging oppressive campus policies and practices.

Many models conclude with descriptions of a stage or phase in which students' focus on this aspect of their identity broadens to include other aspects of their identity, and their approaches to creating social change become more nuanced. In most models, this last stage is not necessarily an ending point, and the passionate intermediate state may be revisited, albeit with greater maturity and complexity, leading to a revised identity.

Later authors (e.g., Jones & McEwen, 2000; McCann & Kim, 2003) pointed out that these models divide complex people into singular aspects of identity, ignoring that our social identities intersect, and that identity is not additive; one cannot adequately understand what it means to be a middle-class Jewish lesbian with a disability by individually considering identity development models of social class, religion, race, ethnicity, sexual orientation, and ability. As it would be impossible to develop models integrating every aspect of every student's social identities, it is important to remember that social identity models are, as are all other models, only partial explanations for complex human phenomena.

Abes, Jones, and McEwen (2007) found that students' understanding of their social identity was further mediated by their epistemological development. How students reason shapes their ability to see, even in themselves, multiple identities simultaneously, with students in earlier stages of development perceiving different aspects of their identity as independent, and more mature students seeing these aspects as inseparable.

APPLYING THEORY IN ACADEMIC AFFAIRS SETTINGS

The models just described, although commonly forming the basis of student affairs work, have numerous implications for many areas of academic affairs. In the pages that follow, I overview a limited number of these implications; many others are possible.

Academic Advising

Academic advisers can foster the development of their advisees in multiple ways. Understanding what issues students are grappling with in their psychosocial lives, how they relate to authority and determine answers, and how they experience their social identities may help us understand why students behave as they do and facilitate movement toward the next developmental position while enabling them to successfully negotiate whatever administrative or academic challenge they face.

Pizzolato (2006) studied the academic advising experiences of students who demonstrated high levels of self-authorship. Academic advisers supported this development by encouraging "goal reflection from multiple perspectives: academic, career, and personal" (p. 34) and helping students focus on future concerns, such as long-term fit with a career choice, as well as immediate issues. This enabled students to "learn to anticipate possible obstacles or challenges and . . . make plans to avoid or overcome potential stumbling blocks" (p. 37), enhancing students' ability to think reflectively.

Faculty Development

Faculty frequently are mystified by students' desire to be told the right answer, inability to use evidence to support their arguments, and lack of understanding of why some evidence and conclusions are more credible than others. Faculty often respond positively when taught models of epistemological development; in particular, they appreciate the specific strategies outlined by King and Kitchener (1994), Knefelkamp (1970/1999), Baxter Magolda (1992, 2000, 2001), and Baxter Magolda and King (2004) for students demonstrating particular forms of reasoning.

Faculty can encourage students' more effective reasoning by modeling cognitively complex ways of thinking, analyzing, and arguing. Faculty should explain the history of current thinking: How have ideas changed in response to new information and data? Students can be shown how to analyze and evaluate arguments. Authorities should stress the complexity of socially and personally important problems and the provisional nature of conclusions. As King (2009) argued, "Educators who aspire to promote development as well as content mastery help students understand the basis for their decisions, explore alternative bases and approaches, and consider the criteria used to compare the quality of alternative explanations" (p. 599).

Many faculty are uncomfortable dealing with the sometimes messy and emotional aspects of students' personal lives, and they resist engaging in these areas. However, knowing what challenges students commonly face regarding psychosocial and social identity development may help them recognize these concerns and make appropriate referrals early on. Faculty certainly should know when, how, and to whom to refer students in distress. Understanding the normal developmental changes students experience can give faculty empathy for students and allow them to provide first-line support when students come to them facing developmental challenges.

Curriculum Design

Models developed by Chickering and Reisser (1993), Josselson (1987), and Marcia (1966) all indicate that course work for students early in their undergraduate careers should include a great deal of exploration, particularly of previously unexamined decisions. Degrees should be sequenced, where possible, to permit students to wait until the middle of their academic experience to declare majors, and career tracks requiring early commitment should allow students to examine real professional settings before irrevocable decisions are made.

Courses in the middle of students' undergraduate career should help students consider the meanings and consequences of their dominant and targeted social identities, recognizing that it is unlikely they have explored their dominant social identities and that acknowledgment of privilege requires both cognitive complexity and strong interpersonal development (King & Baxter Magolda, 2005; King & Shuford, 1996). Later course work should help students explore ethical issues related to their field and anticipate how they will negotiate work–life balance and how their chosen fields align with their values and other life commitments (Chickering & Reisser, 1993).

Several of the models reviewed in this chapter (e.g., Baxter Magolda, 1992; King & Kitchener, 1994; Perry, 1970) indicate younger students will do better in classes with high levels of structure and clear expectations, including explicit expectations and modeling of desired behaviors. As students move into their senior year, course work should encourage them to build arguments, synthesize across domains, apply information to real-life settings, and make commitments to positions, knowing they are subject to revision.

Diversity and Inclusion Initiatives

Almost all of the theories addressed in this chapter speak in some ways to how to foster students' ability to work effectively with people different from themselves, whether in language, nationality, or forms of social identity discussed earlier. King and Baxter Magolda (2005) argued that the ability to understand and interact effectively with others different from oneself is dependent on intrapersonal, interpersonal, and cognitive development. They wrote that earlier

> levels of cognitive and intrapersonal (identity) development may hinder one's
> ability to use one's intercultural skills. Similarly, having a sense of identity

driven predominantly by others' expectations may diminish one's capacity to apply cognitive and interpersonal attributes in intercultural contexts. (p. 573)

They gave examples of a variety of curricular programs that promote development regarding diversity issues, noting that programs with "experiential components, and emphasis on reflection validate students' ability to craft complex perspectives and situate learning in their experience to engage them at their varying levels of intercultural maturity" (p. 588).

Abes and colleagues (2007) suggested that universities could help students develop more complex understanding of social identities through "the incorporation of experiential and reflective components into identity-based academic courses and co-curricular advising, counseling, and programming" (p. 19). They suggested that in either group or individual settings, learning about social identity happens

> where multiple truths about identity perceptions are assumed; [and] students bring their own identity-based experiences and stories into the mix to co-construct with peers, advisors, counselors, and instructors new truths, understandings, and perspectives about their sense of self. (p. 19)

Academic Honesty Policies

Although academic honesty is the obvious place in which theories of moral development have application, both Kohlberg's and Gilligan's models help us understand more global issues, including how students understand what is fair and where responsibilities lie in academic contexts. Kohlberg's model and, in particular, neo-Kohlbergian models have been used to explain cheating behavior as a lack of principled moral reasoning (Wideman, 2011). However, other research has indicated rates of academic dishonesty in students using principled reasoning indistinguishable from those using earlier forms of moral reasoning (e.g., Cummings, Maddux, Harlow, & Dyas, 2002).

Gilligan's model helps us understand students who choose to meet the interests of others at detriment to themselves, including making decisions to leave school, to choose majors that they are not interested in, or to refuse to name peers who are cheating. Juujärvi's (2005, 2006) research indicated students may view helping peers not as academic dishonesty but as expressions of care. Clearly explaining what constitutes cheating and plagiarism and why and particularly addressing what kinds of collaborative work are acceptable may help reduce incidents of academic dishonesty for students who are making moral choices from the middle stages of both Gilligan's and Kohlberg's models.

Career Counseling

Chickering and Reisser (1993) posited that before students can substantively consider questions about their purpose in life, they must come to some initial level of mastery of physical, manual, and intellectual competence; emotions; and interdependence and begin to establish their identity. That this level of development typically does not occur early in students' college career does not imply that career counseling should be deferred to the final years of college. However, it does remind us that a commitment made early in students' college career might well change and that refusal to consider new options may be as much a result of foreclosure (Josselson, 1987) or preoccupation with earlier vectors (Chickering & Reisser, 1993) as of thoughtful consideration. Developmental theories support the idea of encouraging students to explore multiple options during their early college careers. It is reasonable to expect students to change their minds multiple times, and unconsidered commitment should be challenged.

CONCLUSION

Theories and models are, inherently, simplifications of complex phenomena, and the models described here will not explain every action of every student. It is impossible to simultaneously maximize accuracy, simplicity, and generality (Thorngate, 1976). In addition, there are many models not addressed here, particularly those addressing spirituality and faith development, models of learning style and career choice, and other nondevelopmental models that help to explain student behavior. I hope readers use this chapter as a start and expand their knowledge of student development theories, particularly exploring those that speak most directly to the students whose success they seek to foster.

REFERENCES

Abes, E. S., Jones, S. R., & McEwen, M. K. (2007). Reconceptualizing the model of multiple dimensions of identity: The role of meaning-making capacity in the construction of multiple identities. *Journal of College Student Development, 48*, 1–22. doi:10.1353/csd.2007.0000

Association of American Colleges and Universities. (2007). *College learning for the new global century: A report from the national leadership council for liberal education and America's promise.* Washington, DC: Author.

Baxter Magolda, M. B. (1992). *Knowing and reasoning in college: Gender-related patterns in students' intellectual development.* San Francisco, CA: Jossey-Bass.

Baxter Magolda, M. B. (1998). Developing self-authorship in young adult life. *Journal of College Student Development, 39*(2), 143–156.

Baxter Magolda, M. B. (2000). *Teaching to promote intellectual and personal maturity: Incorporating students' worldviews and identities into the learning process.* San Francisco, CA: Jossey-Bass.

Baxter Magolda, M. B. (2001). *Making their own way: Narratives for transforming higher education to promote self-development.* Sterling, VA: Stylus.

Baxter Magolda, M. B. (2008). Three elements of self-authorship. *Journal of College Student Development, 49*(4), 269–284. doi:10.1353/csd.0.0016

Baxter Magolda, M. B. (2009). *Authoring your life: Developing an internal voice to navigate life's challenges.* Sterling, VA: Stylus.

Baxter Magolda, M. B., & King, P. M. (2004). *Learning partnerships: Theory and models of practice to educate for self-authorship.* Sterling, VA: Stylus.

Belenky, M. F., Clinchy, B. M., Goldberger, N. R., & Tarule, J. M. (1986). *Women's ways of knowing: The development of self, voice, and mind.* New York, NY: Basic Books.

Burchell, M., & Broido, E. M. (1995, March). *Toward an integrated theory of social identity development.* Paper presented at the American College Personnel Association conference, Boston, MA.

Chickering, A. W. (1969). *Education and identity.* San Francisco, CA: Jossey-Bass.

Chickering, A. W., & Reisser, L. (1993). *Education and identity* (2nd ed.). San Francisco, CA: Jossey-Bass.

Cummings, R., Maddux, C. D., Harlow, S., & Dyas, L. (2002). Academic misconduct in undergraduate teacher education students and its relationship to their principled moral reasoning. *Journal of Instructional Psychology, 29*(4), 286–296.

Endicott, L., Bock, T., & Narvaez, D. (2003). Moral reasoning, intercultural development, and multicultural experiences: Relations and cognitive underpinnings. *International Journal of Intercultural Relations, 27,* 403–419. doi:10.1016/S0147-1767(03)00030-0

Eriksen, K. (2007). Counseling the "imperial" client: Translating Robert Kegan. *The Family Journal, 15*(2), 174–182. doi:10.1177/1066480706298919

Erikson, E. H. (1959). Identity and the life cycle. *Psychological Issues, 1,* 1–171.

Erikson, E. H. (1968). *Identity: Youth and crisis.* New York, NY: Norton.

Evans, N. J., Forney, D. S., Guido, F. M., Patton, L. D., & Renn, K. A. (2010). *Student development in college: Theory, research, and practice* (2nd ed.). San Francisco, CA: Jossey-Bass.

Gilligan, C. (1977). In a different voice: Women's conception of self and of morality. *Harvard Educational Review, 47*(4), 481–517.

Gilligan, C. (1982). *In a different voice: Psychological theory and women's development.* Cambridge, MA: Harvard University.

Gilligan, C. (1993). *In a different voice: Psychological theory and women' development.* Cambridge, MA: Harvard University. (Original work published 1982)

Hamrick, F. A., Evans, N. J., & Schuh, J. H. (2002). *Foundations of student affairs practice: How philosophy, theory, and research strengthen educational outcomes.* San Francisco, CA: Jossey-Bass.

Jones, S. R., & McEwen, M. K. (2000). A conceptual model of multiple dimensions of identity. *Journal of College Student Development, 41,* 405–414.

Josselson, R. E. (1987). *Finding herself: Pathways to identity development in women.* San Francisco, CA: Jossey-Bass.

Josselson, R. (1996). *Revising herself: The story of women's identity from college to midlife.* New York, NY: Oxford University Press.

Juujärvi, S. (2005). Care and justice in real-life moral reasoning. *Journal of Adult Development, 12*(4), 199–210. doi:10.1007/s10804-005-7088-7

Juujärvi, S. (2006). The ethic of care development: A longitudinal study of moral reasoning among practical-nursing, social-work, and law-enforcement students. *Scandinavian Journal of Psychology, 47*(3), 193–202.

Kegan, R. (1982). *The evolving self.* Cambridge, MA: Harvard University Press.

Kegan, R. (1994). *In over our heads: The mental demands of modern life.* Cambridge, MA: Harvard University Press.

King, P. M. (2009). Principles of development and developmental change underlying theories of cognitive and moral development [50th anniversary issue]. *Journal of College Student Development, 50*(6), 597–620. doi:10.1353/csd.0.0104

King, P. M., & Baxter Magolda, M. B. (2005). A developmental model of intercultural maturity. *Journal of College Student Development, 46*(6), 571–592. doi:10.1353/csd.2005.0060

King, P. M., & Baxter Magolda, M. B. (2011). Student learning. In J. H. Schuh, S. R. Jones, S. R. Harper, & Associates (Eds.), *Student services: A handbook for the profession* (pp. 207–225). San Francisco, CA: Jossey-Bass.

King, P. M., & Kitchener, K. S. (1994). *Developing reflective judgment: Understanding and promoting intellectual growth and critical thinking in adolescents and adults.* San Francisco, CA: Jossey-Bass.

King, P. M., & Shuford, B. C. (1996). A multicultural view is a more cognitively complex view: Cognitive development and multicultural education. *American Behavioral Scientist, 40*(2), 153–164. doi:10.1177/000276429604000205

Kitchener, K. S., & King, P. M. (1981). Reflective judgment: Concepts of justification and their relationship to age and education. *Journal of Applied Developmental Psychology, 2*(2), 89–116. doi:10.1016/0193-3973(81)90032-0

Kitchener, K. S., & King, P. M. (1990). The reflective judgment model: Transforming assumptions about knowing. In J. Mesirow & Associates (Eds.), *Fostering critical reflection in adulthood: A guide to transformative and emancipatory learning* (pp. 157–176). San Francisco, CA: Jossey-Bass.

Knefelkamp, L. L. (1999). Introduction. In W. G. Perry (Ed.), *Forms of ethical and intellectual development in the college years: A scheme.* San Francisco, CA: Jossey-Bass. (Original work published 1970)

Kohlberg, L. (1976). Moral stages and moralization: The cognitive-developmental approach. In T. Likona (Ed.), *Moral development and behavior: Theory, research, and social issues* (pp. 31–53). New York, NY: Holt, Rinehart & Winston.

Kohlberg, L. (1984). *Essays on moral development: Vol. II. The nature and validity of moral stages.* San Francisco, CA: Harper & Row.

Lounsbury, J. W., Huffstetler, B. C., Leong, F. T. L., & Gibson, L. W. (2005). Sense of identity and collegiate academic achievement. *Journal of College Student Development, 46*(5), 501–514. doi:10.1353/csd.2005.0051

Love, P. G., & Guthrie, V. L. (1999). *Understanding and applying cognitive development theory: New directions for student services, No. 88.* San Francisco, CA: Jossey-Bass.

Marcia, J. E. (1966). Development and validation of ego identity status. *Journal of Personality and Social Psychology, 3*, 551–558. doi:10.1037/h0023281

Mayhew, M. J., & King, P. M. (2008). How curricular content and pedagogical strategies affect moral reasoning development in college students. *Journal of Moral Education, 37*(1), 17–40. doi:10.1080/03057240701803668

Mayhew, M. J., Seifert, T. A., & Pascarella, E. T. (2010). A multi-institutional assessment of moral reasoning among first-year students. *The Review of Higher Education, 30*(3), 357–390. doi:10.1353/rhe.0.0153

McCann, C. R., & Kim, S. (2003). *Feminist theory reader: Local and global perspectives.* New York, NY: Routledge.

Perry, W. G. (1970). *Forms of intellectual and ethical development in the college years: A scheme.* New York, NY: Holt, Rinehart & Winston.

Piaget, J. (1952). *The origins of intelligence in children.* New York, NY: International Universities Press.

Pizzolato, J. E. (2006). Complex partnerships: Self-authorship and provocative academic-advising practices. *NACADA Journal, 40*(1), 32–45.

Reed, D. R. C. (1997). *Following Kohlberg: Liberalism and the practice of democratic community.* Notre Dame, IN: University of Notre Dame Press.

Rest, J. R. (1986). *Moral development: Advances in research and theory.* New York, NY: Praeger.

Skoe, E. E. (1998). Ethic of care: Issues in moral development. In E. E. Skoe & A. L. von der Lippe (Eds.), *Personality development in adolescence: A cross-national and life-span perspective.* London, UK: Routledge.

Thorngate, W. (1976). "In general" vs. "it depends": Some comments of the Gergen-Schlenker debate. *Personality and Social Psychology Bulletin, 2*(4), 404–410. doi:10.1177/014616727600200413

Torres, V. (2011). Perspectives on identity development. In J. H. Schuh, S. R. Jones, S. R. Harper, & S. R. Komives (Eds.), *Student services: A handbook for the profession* (pp. 187–206). San Francisco, CA: Jossey-Bass.

Torres, V., Jones, S. R., & Renn, K. A. (2009). Identity development theories in student affairs: Origins, current status, and new approaches. *Journal of College Student Development, 50*(6), 577–596. doi:10.1353/csd.0.0102

Wideman, M. (2011). Caring or collusion? Academic dishonesty in a school of nursing. *Canadian Journal of Higher Education, 41*(2), 28–43.

3

Diversity in Higher Education

Nancy J. Evans and James DeVita

T HE MODERN INSTITUTION OF higher education enrolls students from a diverse range of backgrounds and experiences. Students from different racial identities, socioeconomic statuses, religious affiliations, and educational experiences can be found on every college campus in the United States. Diversity, in terms of both students served and institutional mission and type supported, is a hallmark of American higher education (e.g., Gurin, Dey, Hurtado, & Gurin, 2004; Hirt, 2006; Hurtado, 2003; Thelin, 2004). Indeed, using these critera the United States boasts the most diverse system of higher education in the world. In this chapter, we discuss the implications of diversity in higher education, examining the meaning of diversity, ways in which diversity affects the modern college, impact of diversity in the classroom, issues to consider when working with students from diverse backgrounds, and considerations in the design of a multicultural curriculum.

MEANING OF DIVERSITY

Institutions of higher education provide spaces for students to experience diversity both inside and outside of the classroom. Although "we may not know for years that a single lecture or conversation or experience started a chain reaction that transformed some aspect of ourselves . . . [or] easily discern what subtle mix of people, books, settings, or events promotes growth"

61

(Chickering & Reisser, 1993, p. 43), it is clear that the experiences students have during college profoundly affect their personal and educational development (Chickering & Reisser, 1993; Evans, Forney, Guido, Patton, & Renn, 2010; Pascarella & Terenzini, 2005). Chickering and Reisser (1993) identified several aspects of identity that often change during college. These components highlight the significance of understanding diversity:

> (1) comfort with body and appearance, (2) comfort with gender and sexual orientation, (3) sense of self in a social, historical, and cultural context, (4) clarification of self-concept through roles and life-style, (5) sense of self in response to feedback from valued others, (6) self-acceptance and self-esteem, and (7) personal stability and integration. (p. 49)

Students' development does not begin when students arrive on a college campus; rather, there are numerous experiences within and beyond their educational experiences that shape who they are, their sense of self, and how they interact with and relate to others (Chickering & Reisser, 1993; Evans et al., 2010; Pascarella & Terenzini, 2005). Regardless of the identities with which students arrive at college, they are exposed to individuals who represent different identities and faculty and staff who share new ideas and concepts. In addition, students participate in experiences that expose them to diverse aspects of various cultures. Thus, it is critical to understand the ways in which diversity affects all college students.

Although it is important to understand the effects associated with diversity for all college students (Astin, 1999; Chickering & Reisser, 1993; Pascarella & Terenzini, 2005), it is equally important to acknowledge that college campuses have historically excluded some individuals (e.g., racial and ethnic minorities [REMs] and women), while privileging those who are White, Christian, male, heterosexual, and able-bodied (Chang, Milem, & antonio, 2011). When compared to their peers, students who have been historically excluded (i.e., marginalized populations) are likely to encounter unique challenges that are related, in part, to the marginalization that individuals who embody nondominant identities face in society. Women and REMs, for example, were once excluded from higher education altogether or provided separate institutions with disparate opportunities that mirrored their access, or lack thereof, to rights and resources in the United States (e.g., Altbach, Berdahl, & Gumport, 2005). Other groups, like lesbian, gay, bisexual, and transgender (LGBT) individuals; persons with disabilities; and individuals affiliated with nondominant religions, experience more subtle forms of discrimination that perpetuate their exclusion from campus life. Although these individuals may not be explicitly denied access, campuses that fail to develop inclusive policies essentially exclude them.

DIVERSITY ON THE MODERN COLLEGE CAMPUS

As previously alluded to, diversity refers to both the various identities that individuals bring with them and develop during their time on campus and the diversity present among institutions of higher education in the United States. Although this chapter focuses on the unique issues and opportunities associated with academic support of diverse students, administrators should also understand the ways in which students experience the climate associated with their institutional type and mission. Student backgrounds and characteristics have a reciprocal relationship with the environment present on campus (Banning, 1978). Simply put, individual and institutional diversity affect each other in meaningful and unpredictable ways.

Personal Identities

There are many aspects of an individual that may be celebrated when defining *diversity*. Age, gender, race and ethnicity, citizenship status, ability, social class, sexual orientation, gender identity, and religious affiliation are among the many identities that influence students' experiences. Issues to consider when working with students from these specific backgrounds will be discussed in greater detail in the following sections. Undoubtedly there are other identities that administrators should consider, some of which may be more salient to students than those discussed here. We chose to focus on these personal identities in part because of the pervasive climate associated with American higher education, rooted in its historical mission to educate elite, White males in preparation for service in the clergy (Rudolph, 1962).

Although the college campus looked very different by the twentieth century than it did when Harvard was chartered in 1636 (Rudolph, 1962), student diversity did not truly explode until the mid- to late 1960s. By 1970, open access to college provided nontraditionally aged students, women, REMs, and students with disabilities the opportunity to attend college in greater numbers (e.g., Hirt, 2006). In the past 40 years, student diversity has continued to increase. In 1970, there were approximately 8.5 million students enrolled in degree-granting institutions; institutions were predominantly male (59%) and White (83%) with students enrolled full-time (68%). Just a decade later, women had overtaken men for the highest percentage of undergraduate enrollment (the graduate enrollment of women was higher by 1988), and by 2009, REMs represented more than two thirds of all college students (U.S. Department of Education, National Center for Education Statistics, 2011a). In addition, statistics reported by the U.S. Department of Education from 2007–2008 indicate that students with disabilities (approximately 11%), students with "non-resident alien" status (3.5%), and students over age 24 years (46%) are well represented on college campuses across the country (U.S. Department of Education, National Center for Education Statistics, 2011b). Beyond the identities that are quantified by education statistics, we also chose to include LGBT-identified students, students from lower socioeconomic classes, and students affiliated with nondominant religions because of their growing presence and visibility on college campuses and our desire to give voice to their experiences.

Institutional Diversity

Similar to the ways in which students enrolled in college have changed over time, the types and missions of higher education institutions have evolved along a related trajectory. The foci of education have shifted dramatically across institutional environments. Research-focused institutions, for example, place greater emphasis on graduate education and faculty research than do liberal arts institutions that endeavor to promote the holistic development of undergraduate students (Hirt, 2006). Specialized institutions, such as historically Black colleges and universities (HBCU), Hispanic-serving institutions (HSI), women's colleges, and religiously affiliated institutions, often serve a mission similar to that of liberal arts institutions but provide specialized supports that align with their unique mission and student body (Hirt, 2006; Merisotis & O'Brien, 1998). Although community colleges are also focused on development, they are typically responsive to the demands of a market-based economy within a localized community (Hirt, 2006). Tribal colleges, most of which are two-year colleges, are similar in many ways to community colleges yet also have unique missions related to educating their Native American students. This brief summary of institutional types that thrive in the American system of higher education does not adequately honor the diversity that exists.

Each type of institution provides opportunities and obstacles to addressing issues of diversity on campus. For example, collaborative support is institutionalized at liberal arts colleges, whereas research institutions often struggle to create smaller communities among large numbers of undergraduate students. Community colleges may have difficulty forming a community because of a large number of nontraditional students and an ever-changing population of students and faculty members. These differences have a real impact on students' experiences in the classroom, which academic administrators need to be aware of to meet the needs of a diverse student population.

IMPACT OF DIVERSITY IN THE CLASSROOM

Diverse students have diverse needs in the classroom. They bring with them different backgrounds, experiences, values, pressures, and interests. Their goals for being in college vary, and the ways in which they learn best are also diverse (El-Khawas, 2003).

The dynamics of privilege and oppression are played out in the classroom in a number of ways. Being a member of an oppressed group can affect a student's learning by adding stresses and issues that other students do not face (e.g., Guardia & Evans, 2008a; Jehangir, 2010; Renn, 2004). Learning styles of diverse populations often vary, requiring different teaching strategies (e.g., J. A. Anderson & Adams, 1992; Cuyjet & Associates, 2006; Yamazaki, 2005). In addition, various cultural groups weigh the value of education for their youth differently, placing increased pressure on students to do well (e.g., Jehangir, 2010).

Similar to society as a whole, inequities among student populations are often present in the classroom. Communication barriers, classroom arrangements, and student and faculty attitudes toward particular groups often present challenges for certain students, whereas other students are rarely aware of these barriers (e.g., Connolly, 2000; Evans, Assadi, & Herriott, 2005; Hecht, Jung, & Wadsworth, 2008).

Another factor that is often lacking for students from diverse backgrounds is a feeling of inclusion in the classroom (e.g., Ali & Bagheri, 2009; Harper & Hurtado, 2007; Hecht et al., 2008). Because a student from a diverse background is often the only student or one of a very few students from an identity group, he, she, or ze (gender neutral pronoun) can feel alone and unwelcomed. These feelings can result from the personal treatment these students receive in the classroom or from a lack of inclusion of material in the course content relevant to their group. We discuss each of these factors in the sections following.

How Nondominant Group Membership Affects Learning

Students' backgrounds affect their learning in a number of different ways. In particular, students who are members of nondominant populations have experiences in the classroom that are different from those of students who come from privileged backgrounds. Competing issues, learning styles, and perceptions of the value of education vary depending on the students' social identities and the self-perceptions, values, and experiences that accompany those identities.

Competing issues. Students lead full lives, of which their classroom experiences are only a part. Being a college student in the United States can be an unfamiliar and overwhelming experience for individuals from nondominant backgrounds (G. Anderson, Carmichael, Harper, & Huang, 2009; Jehangir, 2010). They are often entering into new environments with individuals who are quite different from them in terms of values, experiences, and goals. They also experience marginalization and isolation that students from dominant groups generally do not. Students who are members of oppressed groups are often victims of stereotypes, prejudice, and harassment. All of these factors can interfere in significant ways with their classroom performance (Chang et al., 2011; Connolly, 2000; Hurtado, Milem, Clayton-Petersen, & Allen, 1999; Jehangir, 2010; Maxwell & Shammas, 2008; Pascarella, Pierson, Wolniak, & Terenzini, 2004).

For example, if a gay male student is being harassed by his roommate or other students on his residence hall floor, it will be hard for him to study and focus on his class work (Evans & Broido, 1999). Similarly, a first-generation student whose parents never attended college is unaware of the resources available to her on campus and may be intimidated by a class of 500 students (Jehangir, 2010). She may feel totally lost and have no idea how to cope with an environment that is completely new to her or whom to ask for assistance if she is struggling with class assignments.

Learning styles. Student learning is obviously the central goal of the college experience, but students learn in different ways. Yamazaki (2005) found that culture influences learning styles and needs to be considered in working with students from different countries, whereas J. A. Anderson and Adams (1992) discovered differences in learning styles related to gender and ethnicity.

Learning styles influence how well students respond to specific teaching techniques and how they perform in different academic areas (Kolb, 1981).

Thus, students whose types do not "match" those of the majority of students in a field may have a difficult time understanding and succeeding in that field or in a class in that area.

Value of education. The extent to which families and cultures value education can affect students positively or negatively. First-generation students who come from families in which working is considered more important than education often lack the support they need to succeed in an unfamiliar environment and struggle with feelings of guilt for not contributing needed income to their families (Jehangir, 2009; Pizzolato, 2003). For example, Latino/a students, particularly women, sometimes have to fight to attend college rather than stay home to care for their families (Ortiz & Santos, 2009). On the other hand, many students of color who are the first in their communities to go to college can feel the weight of the entire community's expectation to do well (Jehangir, 2009). International students, whose families sacrifice to send their children to the United States to earn valued degrees, can also experience enormous pressure to succeed (G. Anderson et al., 2009).

Inequities in the Classroom

Both the physical construction of the classroom and the attitudes expressed by other students or faculty can create an inequitable environment for students from nondominant populations. For instance, a tiered classroom with bolted-down chairs doesn't leave space for a student who uses a wheelchair (Evans et al., 2005). Classrooms decorated with pictures or other artifacts that represent only White culture can cause students from other racial and ethnic backgrounds to feel left out and devalued (Ortiz & Santos, 2009). Hearing derogatory comments about a gay character in a novel can lead LGBT students to feel unsafe and unwelcome in a classroom (Connolly, 2000). Having a test scheduled on a major religious holiday for Muslim, Jewish, or other non-Christian students discounts the importance of their religious traditions, while having a three-week vacation over the Christian holiday of Christmas indicates which beliefs are valued and which are not (Seifert, 2007).

Feeling Unwelcome and Unwanted

Students perform best in classrooms in which they feel welcomed and included (Rendón, 1994; Schlossberg, 1989). Unfortunately, many members of nondominant groups often feel excluded from class activities and uncomfortable expressing their opinions because of the actions and words of students and faculty who are from the dominant group (e.g., Ali & Bagheri, 2009; Connolly, 2000; Harper & Hurtado, 2007; Jehangir, 2009). Failure to see oneself represented in readings and class discussion also contributes to feelings of exclusion (e.g., Connolly, 2000; Jehangir, 2009; Nichols & Quaye, 2009).

Personal treatment. Often unconsciously, students who are not members of the dominant group are ignored or treated unfairly in the classroom (e.g., Ali & Bagheri, 2009; Connolly, 2000; Nichols & Quaye, 2009). For example, small group work completed outside of class may be very difficult to schedule for a single mother with small children (Silverman, Aliabadi, & Stiles, 2009). Being asked to meet with her group at 9:00 p.m. in a residence hall is likely to make her feel that her situation is not being taken into consideration and that others are unwilling to adjust to accommodate her time limitations. Members of racial and ethnic groups are often asked to speak for their group, putting them on the spot and unfairly singling them out when in reality they can present only their own individual opinions (Solórzano, Ceja, & Yosso, 2000).

Inclusion in course content. Not seeing or hearing anything about one's group in course content can be very exclusionary. Textbooks and other assigned reading in classes rarely address issues related to disability (Nichols & Quaye, 2009) or sexual orientation (Connolly, 2000)—even in courses in which such content would be relevant, such as history, sociology, or psychology. In technical or scientific areas, where less directly relevant content exists, failure to use inclusive examples or to include material written by authors from various populations is noticed, and students feel ignored and irrelevant.

ISSUES TO CONSIDER WHEN WORKING WITH VARIOUS POPULATIONS

In addition to the issues that affect students from a variety of backgrounds, each student identity group also faces unique issues. In this section, we discuss factors that affect adult students, women, students with minoritized racial and ethnic identities, international students, students with disabilities, students from lower social class backgrounds, LGBT students, students affiliated with nondominant religions, and students with multiple identities.

Adults

Adult college students encounter numerous challenges when they enroll in higher education, including balancing their various existing responsibilities (family, financial, personal) with the demands of life as a student (e.g., Deutsch & Schmertz, 2011; Hardin, 2008). These competing responsibilities force adult students to carefully consider expenditures of money and time prior to and during their enrollment in college (Frey, 2007). Further complicating adult students' experience in higher education is a diminished confidence in their academic abilities associated with having been out of school for an extended period of time or having performed poorly when they were last enrolled (e.g., Zemke & Zemke, 1995). The adult student experience in higher education is best characterized as a multilayered negotiation among a seemingly endless list of concerns.

Colleges and universities can meet the needs of adult learners by providing flexible opportunities. The mutable nature of community colleges has traditionally provided such opportunities for adult students (Frey, 2007) by offering courses on weekends and evenings and providing clear program requirements that enhance practical skills and ease transition to four-year institutions. Academic administrators at all institutions could consider using technology to provide course offerings that are more efficient in terms of both financial resources and time. Faculty members and academic advisers should offer adult students feedback that not only is supportive but also helps adult students avoid duplicating efforts or completing courses that will not help them achieve their goals. Academic administrators should take a holistic approach to supporting adult learners by encouraging them to regularly clarify their goals and discuss their personal obligations through a process of facilitated exploration (Zemke & Zemke, 1995). Peer support groups and other resources readily accessible to adult students (e.g., online discussion boards and blogs) should be made available.

Women

Although female college students now represent the majority of students enrolled in higher education (U.S. Department of Education, National Center for Education Statistics, 2011a), college campuses remain male-dominated institutions. It is well established that women experience "chilly" climates both within and beyond the classroom, encountering sexism and diminished expectations, among other negative experiences (e.g., R. M. Hall & Sandler, 1984; Morris & Daniel, 2008). In response to negative climates, female college students are typically more reliant on personal relationships with family members and peers than their male counterparts and report higher levels of stress related to their academic success (e.g., Rayle & Chung, 2008). The lack of female mentors, particularly in fields in which women have been traditionally underrepresented, exacerbates academic stress (e.g., Gunasekera & Friedrich, 2009; Morris & Daniel, 2008). Despite the negative environment, at least one study found that women enrolled in more credit hours than men and achieved higher grade point averages (Clifton, Perry, Roberts, & Peter, 2008).

Although female college students appear to be better equipped for success than other nondominant groups, it is important for academic administrators and faculty members to be aware of persistent inequities that exist in the classroom. Initiatives aimed at encouraging faculty members to address these inequities should be supported by administrators. Women represent the majority of students enrolled on many college campuses but maintain a limited presence in certain fields of study (e.g., science, mathematics, and engineering). Thus, administrators should develop programs that provide women with supportive networks of peers, faculty, and professionals in fields where they are traditionally underrepresented. Academic advisers and faculty members must also be aware of the stress that female college students endure and provide support that seeks to ameliorate the negative consequences but does not threaten the academic and professional aspirations of women.

Marginalized REMs

REMs receive disparate learning opportunities throughout their educational experiences that may multiply as they enter and persist in college (e.g., Maple & Stage, 1991; Tate, 2001). Although not all REMs encounter the same issues, overwhelmingly these students are less prepared for success during college (e.g., Greene & Forster, 2003) and more likely to encounter racism and discrimination (e.g., Solórzano et al., 2000; Villalpando, 2004). The issues encountered by REMs on most college campuses are further complicated by the lack of faculty and staff members who share their identities (e.g., Saddler, 2010). Overall, college campuses produce "chilly" climates for REMs that contribute to feelings of isolation and loneliness.

Academic administrators must find ways to create welcoming spaces that celebrate the diversity that REMs bring with them to campus. Administrators should promote and encourage a collaborative approach to learning that integrates extracurricular experiences into the curriculum. By working with student services and organizations that focus on issues encountered by REMs, colleges and universities can provide students with a supportive network of peers and mentors that build connections and create spaces that challenge racism and discrimination perpetuated elsewhere. In addition, a collaborative, community-based approach to learning aligns well with the cultural norms experienced by some REMs (e.g., Strayhorn & Terrell, 2010). To be successful, administrators must (a) encourage the inclusion of issues associated with race, ethnicity, racism, and White privilege into the curriculum; (b) hire and promote individuals with demonstrated success working with REMs on campus; and (c) seek opportunities to work *with* REMs to address issues on campus.

International Students

The internationalization and globalization of higher education is evident in the rise of American students who study abroad and students from other countries who enroll in American institutions. Students from over 150 countries matriculate at American institutions (Institute of International Education, 2010), and they encounter numerous issues that include homesickness, pressure from family members, and cultural dissonance (Hecht et al., 2008). In addition, misunderstandings associated with faculty–student expectations and challenges between home and campus cultures provide added obstacles to the success of international students (G. Anderson et al., 2009). The challenges encountered by international students can leave them feeling as if they are alone, disconnected from the dominant culture.

Academic administrators should develop opportunities for international and American students to engage with one another in meaningful ways. International students bring unique perspectives that enhance learning and provide opportunities for cross-cultural understanding. American students would greatly benefit from classrooms and academic experiences that honor different perspectives. Administrators are charged with the difficult task of creating a campus community that celebrates the diverse cultures associated with its international students.

Students With Disabilities

Students with disabilities are a heterogeneous group that represents various differences in ability, including mobility, hearing, visual, learning, and speech, among others. Students with disabilities are often left to advocate for themselves to counter stereotypes that they are lazy or lack motivation (e.g., French, 2000; Sparks & Lovett, 2009). Unfortunately, for students with disabilities, success in college is often dependent on an ability to self-advocate that many students with disabilities never develop (Abreu-Ellis, Ellis, & Hayes, 2009; Evans & Economos, 2010). One impediment to students' success is the continuous exposure to microaggressions that students with disabilities encounter, ultimately relegating them to second-class status on campus (Ryan & Scura, 2011).

Academic administrators and faculty members must be aware of the invisibility of many student disabilities across campus and in the class-room. Although we tend to think of students with visible disabilities, such as mobility or visual impairments, the majority of students with disabilities have impairments that are not readily visible, such as learning disabilities or psychiatric impairments (L. M. Hall & Belch, 2000). Students should be encouraged to discuss their different abilities in class assignments, and once academic administrators are aware of the unique experiences of students with disabilities, they should advocate for their consideration in policies, programs, and curricula. Because negative attitudes of others, invisibility, and self-advocacy are major issues that students with disabilities encounter, administrators should find ways to give these students a voice.

Students From Less Privileged Social Class Backgrounds

Similar to REMs, low-income students when compared to their middle- and high-income peers are provided with disparate learning opportunities and diminished cultural capital (e.g., Martinez & Kloppott, 2003, 2005). Students from low-income families may lack access to information about college and work; choose to hide their socioeconomic status from their middle- and upper-class peers; and be forced to work while attending college to pay for tuition, books, and living expenses (e.g., Duffy, 2007; Oldfield, 2007; Ostrove & Love, 2007). The lack of access to resources may mean that students from lower social class backgrounds miss opportunities for professional and personal development, such as study abroad experiences and summer internships.

To create environments that are inclusive of students from lower-income backgrounds, academic administrators should carefully consider how financial constraints might limit the engagement of students in supplemental educational experiences. Experiences that range from an evening film or lecture series to study abroad opportunities might prevent students who have to work or rely on financial aid from participating. Faculty members and administrators should be prepared to offer alternative experiences or specialized funding sources to support students from lower-income backgrounds. Technological resources could provide enhanced opportunities for learning and engagement that are inexpensive or even free, as well as accommodate a variety of schedules.

Lesbian, Gay, Bisexual, and Transgender Students

LGBT students on college campuses have encountered stigma related to their identity that has often relegated them to marginalized status in society. The pervasive climate around sexual orientation and gender identity keeps many LGBT college students "closeted" and halts the developmental process at self-disclosure, at best (D'Augelli, 1994; Rhoads, 1994). Rhoads (1994) concluded, "Little has changed. [LGBT] students still face harassment and discrimination, and their experiences are still largely excluded from the classroom" (p. 35). Over two decades later, his statement accurately reflects the general landscape for LGBT students on many, if not all, college campuses.

There are numerous issues academic administrators should consider when working with LGBT students. Administrators should allow LGBT individuals to define their identities by asking all students to self-disclose how they conceptualize their sexual orientation and gender identity and select the pronouns they prefer to use. Promoting inclusive academic experiences is also important; for example, faculty members should be encouraged to include LGBT-focused topics, readings, and examples in their courses and be amenable when students raise questions about LGBT issues. Participation in educational programming (e.g., Safe Zone trainings) that provides a symbol or placard that can be displayed indicates to students that an administrator is willing to consider the needs of LGBT students (Evans, 2002). Simply put, academic administrators should find ways to indicate that they are willing to serve as a resource for LGBT students; otherwise, students are likely to remain closeted and distanced from administrators and faculty.

Students Affiliated With Nondominant Religions

Despite the explicit inclusion of religious freedom among the rights guaranteed to Americans, social institutions, including institutions of higher education, perpetuate the privilege and dominance of Christian religions in their policies and practices (Beyer, 2003). Academic calendars and religious celebrations are organized around Christian traditions, ignoring the practices of other religions. Students affiliated with non-Christian religions experience isolation and dietary restrictions and are faced with campus facilities that do not align with their religious practices (e.g., mixed-sex housing options). In addition, hostility toward unfamiliar religious traditions, particularly Islam, has increased significantly (e.g., Mahaffey & Smith, 2009).

Perhaps the easiest step that academic administrators can take to support students from nondominant religions is to notify faculty, staff, and students about policies that provide accommodations for expectations on religious holidays and remind the campus community as those dates approach. Careful consideration should be given to the timing of critical dates in the academic calendar to avoid conflicts whenever possible. Identifying mentors and communities of support for students from nondominant religions would also be meaningful (Mahaffey & Smith, 2009). Finally, flexibility in policies that provide accommodations to students to practice and live their faith both inside and beyond the classroom is crucial.

Multiple Identities and Intersectionality

Because college is a place where individuals experience significant growth in terms of various dimensions of their identity development, it is important to be aware of the identity (or identities) that are most salient to students at various points during their time on campus (Chickering & Reisser, 1993; Evans et al., 2010; Pascarella & Terenzini, 2005). Often the saliency of identity is directly associated with the environment in which development is occurring. For example, a study of African American gay male college students found that despite experiencing racism in LGBT-inclusive spaces, African American gay male college students were more comfortable among their LGBT peers than their African American peers (Strayhorn et al., 2008). This preference was primarily because their status as a racial minority on a predominantly White campus forced spaces focused on African American identity to celebrate race at the expense of other identities that individuals within those spaces believed were significant. For the African American gay males in this study, racial identity development was suspended as they examined their sexual orientation.

This example illustrates the ways in which multiple identities intersect in meaningful ways for students. Although we have provided an overview of issues to consider when working with specific populations, academic administrators must avoid assuming that an obvious identity (e.g., race, gender, ability) is more salient to a student than a hidden identity (e.g., sexual orientation, social class, religious affiliation). Indeed, most students are negotiating multiple, competing identities within multiple contexts across campus (Abes, Jones, & McEwen, 2007; Jones & McEwen, 2000).

Beyond understanding how individuals negotiate their multiple identities, it is crucial that administrators consider how the policies and practices enacted in institutions perpetuate systems of oppression. The concept of intersectionality, first developed by Crenshaw (1994), argues that discrimination experienced by Black women is based not on race only or gender only but on the inextricable relationship between those two aspects of identity. Academic administrators are left with the admittedly daunting responsibility of considering the ways in which students with multiple marginalized identities interpret and negotiate policies and practices enacted on campus. Regardless of the homogeneity perceived within a group of students, administrators must realize that within-group heterogeneity is as significant as differences among groups (Harper & Nichols, 2008).

Military-Affiliated and Veteran Students

Although the presence of veteran students on college campuses is not a new phenomenon, the Post-9/11 GI Bill provided an opportunity for veteran students to enroll in higher education at increased rates (McBain, Kim, Cook, & Snead, 2012; Rumann & Hamrick, 2010; Sander, 2012). Higher enrollment rates have raised awareness of the need for better understanding about the issues facing veteran students and the services needed to support them. McBain and colleagues found that 427 of the 690 institutions surveyed provided services and programming for veteran students. Yet, veteran students still encounter many barriers in access to higher education, as well as stressors while enrolled. For example, veteran students have been shown to exhibit high rates of psychological symptoms, including "almost 35% of the sample [in one study] experiencing severe anxiety, 24% experiencing severe depression, and almost 46% evidencing significant symptoms of PTSD" (Rudd, Goulding, & Bryant, 2011, p. 358). Suicide risks are also significant for this population of students, and the alarming rates should lead universities to question their preparedness in supporting veteran students' health (Rudd et al., 2011; Whiteman, Barry, Mroczek, & Wadsworth, 2013). Furthermore, the transition to a dual civilian–student role has also been shown to affect the comfort and engagement of veteran students on campus (e.g., Rumann & Hamrick, 2010). Classified as adult learners or nontraditional students, veteran students may become frustrated in academic settings with traditionally aged undergraduates (i.e., 18–22-year-olds) who are less experienced, lack maturity, and often fail to appreciate the unique experiences of veterans (Ross-Gordon, 2011; Rumann & Hamrick, 2010; Sander, 2012). The intersection of their adult status and military experience makes them likely to "also exhibit varied learning styles and preferences influenced in part by their past encounters with higher education as well as by their social and cultural backgrounds, and are best not seen as a monolithic group" (Ross-Gordon, 2011, p. 5). Rather, programming and services to support veteran students must account for the diversity of experiences and developmental trajectories of this group.

To provide adequate support for veteran students in higher education, academic administrators should integrate staff and programming from a variety of areas that are typically dispersed across campus. Veteran students will likely encounter issues with the enrollment process, beginning with financial aid and advising given their reliance on the Post-9/11 GI Bill for financial support and transient enrollment patterns pre-, during, and postservice in the military (Rumann & Hamrick, 2010; Sander, 2012). In addition, veteran students feel most comfortable among others who have faced similar transitional issues to both civilian and student statuses (e.g., Rumann & Hamrick, 2010). Thus, organizations like the Reserve Officers' Training Corps (ROTC) and other military-affiliated groups that already exist on campus would be meaningful resources with which to connect veteran students for social and academic support. A collaborative effort to support veteran students is most likely to be successful, as veterans need access to specialized health and psychological services, guidance on accessing full educational benefits, support getting integrated into campus life, and academic supports that mirror adult students' needs, among others (Mitstifer, 2012; Rudd et al., 2011; Rumann & Hamrick, 2010). Academic administrators seeking to support veteran students must find ways to engage colleagues from multiple areas across campus (e.g., financial aid, student services, health and counseling centers) and be prepared to develop unique programs tailored for veteran students that ease integration to campus and provide opportunities for academic support. Whenever possible, those efforts should be distinct from those offered to traditional undergraduates and provide access to other veterans or military-affiliated populations.

MULTICULTURAL CURRICULUM

Creating a multicultural curriculum can help to address the issues and needs we have discussed in this chapter. A multicultural curriculum, however, involves more than including a reading or two by people of color or adding a class session on diversity. Developing a welcoming, inclusive environment that is sensitive to diverse students of all backgrounds takes careful planning. Faculty must consider not only the content of the course but also the process. As we have discussed, classroom dynamics play a major role in determining if a classroom experience is positive or negative for students from various backgrounds.

Content

Adding material that is related to different cultures and populations is the most obvious way to address diversity in the classroom (Banks, 1997). Readings, videos, speakers, and other content should reflect the diversity of groups within the global society. Ensuring that issues and ideas that represent diverse populations and points of view are part of classes creates an inclusive and welcoming environment for all students, as well as educates them regarding the diversity of the society in which they live (Adams, 2007). Including authors from different backgrounds is another way to demonstrate support for diverse populations. Even in a class such as chemistry, students notice if the names of the authors of books and articles they are reading are from diverse cultural groups.

If the content of class does not lend itself to the inclusion of multicultural content, examples can be used that reflect diversity. For instance, word problems can use names from various cultures, and situations that are included can acknowledge diverse situations. In a class such as technical theatre, in which students learn to build and light sets, students can be assigned to design and build sets for plays with diverse themes.

Process

All classes can be structured to acknowledge the diversity of students in the classroom (Adams, 2007). Faculty must be aware of bias in class assignments, such as requiring a large amount of out-of-class group work that places undue pressure on working students, parents, and students who commute long distances. In-class teaching techniques, such as showing uncaptioned videos, can disadvantage students with hearing difficulties or those who are deaf. Learning about universal instructional design, which enables all students to participate equally in the class, is a beneficial way to ensure that classroom activities and assignments are equitable (Higbee & Barajas, 2007).

Setting norms of inclusion on the first day of class and reinforcing them if issues arise is another valuable way to enable students to feel welcomed and included (Adams, 2007). Use of inclusive language, both verbal and nonverbal, should be addressed, along with such norms as speaking for oneself and not asking students to represent their identity groups. Teachers also need to demonstrate visible and vocal intolerance of derogatory statements as a way to support students who are being targeted, as well as model respect for all students.

Faculty can also support students by being aware of and sensitive to the outside demands they may be facing (Guardia & Evans, 2008b). For instance, allowing Native American students to miss class to return home for important holidays or family events demonstrates an understanding of the important role of family and community in their culture. Providing extensions on papers or other assignments for students who have to work extra hours to cover unexpected expenses shows an understanding of the demands facing working-class students who must support themselves.

Using universal instructional design principles, teachers can accommodate various learning styles by using a variety of teaching strategies and assignments that require a range of skills (Pliner & Johnson, 2004; Silver, Bourke, & Strehorn, 1998). Presenting assignments in several modalities, such as verbal directions, PowerPoint slides, and written guidelines, can ensure that all students understand what is required. Having assignments that use a range of skills, including oral presentations, written papers, take-home tests, and experiential activities, helps to level the playing field for students, because one assignment may require them to use their strongest skills, whereas the next may use a weaker skill (Forney, 1994). Giving students an opportunity to choose from a variety of assignments is another way to enable them to demonstrate their learning in a manner that is effective for them.

CONCLUSION

As institutions of higher education become more diverse, academic administrators are faced with the challenge of creating environments in which students from a wide variety of backgrounds can be successful. In this chapter, we offered information regarding the issues and needs of various student populations that we hope is helpful to administrators as they work with faculty to prepare them to effectively teach and advise diverse students. Although one chapter certainly cannot fully cover all the differences among students or characteristics of diverse students, the suggestions we provided and the references we cited can be a start in sensitively addressing concerns of many student populations and creating multicultural classrooms and curriculum.

REFERENCES

Abes, E. S., Jones, S. R., & McEwen, M. K. (2007). Reconceptualizing the model of multiple dimensions of identity: The role of meaning-making capacity in the construction of multiple identities. *Journal of College Student Development, 48,* 1–22.

Abreu-Ellis, C., Ellis, J., & Hayes, R. (2009). College preparedness and time of learning disability identification. *Journal of Developmental Education, 32*(3), 28–30.

Adams, M. (2007). Pedagogical frameworks for social justice education. In M. A. Adams, L. A. Bell, & P. Griffin (Eds.), *Teaching for diversity and social justice* (2nd ed., pp.15–33). New York, NY: Routledge.

Ali, S. R., & Bagheri, E. (2009). Practical suggestions to accommodate the needs of Muslim students on campus. In S. K. Watt, E. E. Fairchild, & K. M. Goodman (Eds.), *Intersections of religious privilege: Difficult dialogues and student affairs practice: New directions for student services, No. 125* (pp. 47–54). San Francisco, CA: Jossey-Bass.

Altbach, P. G., Berdahl, R. O., & Gumport, P. J. (Eds.). (2005). *American higher education in the twenty-first century: Social, political, and economic challenges* (2nd ed.). Baltimore, MD: Johns Hopkins University Press.

Anderson, G., Carmichael, K. Y., Harper, T. J., & Huang, T. (2009). International students at four-year institutions: Developmental needs, issues, and strategies. In S. R. Harper & S. J. Quaye (Eds.), *Student engagement in higher education* (pp. 17–37). New York, NY: Routledge.

Anderson, J. A., & Adams, M. (1992). Acknowledging the learning styles of diverse student populations: Implications for instructional design. In L. L. B. Border & N. V. N. Chism (Eds.), *Teaching for diversity: New directions for teaching and learning, No. 49* (pp. 19–33). San Francisco, CA: Jossey-Bass.

Astin, A. W. (1999). Student involvement: A developmental theory for higher education. *Journal of College Student Development, 40*(5), 518–529.

Banks, J. A. (1997). Transformative knowledge, curriculum reform, and action. In J. A. Banks (Ed.), *Multicultural education, transformative knowledge, and action: Historical and contemporary perspectives* (pp. 335–346). New York, NY: Teachers College Press.

Banning, J. H. (1978). *Campus ecology: A perspective for student affairs.* Washington, DC: National Association for Student Personnel Administrators.

Beyer, P. (2003). Constitutional privilege and constituting pluralism: Religious freedom in national, global, and legal context. *Journal for the Scientific Study of Religion, 42*(3), 333–339.

Chang, M. J., Milem, J. F., & antonio, a. l. (2011). Campus climate and diversity. In J. H. Schuh, S. R. Jones, S. R. Harper, & Associates (Eds.), *Student services: A handbook for the profession* (5th ed., pp. 43–58). San Francisco, CA: Jossey-Bass.

Chickering, A. W., & Reisser, L. (1993). *Education and identity* (2nd ed.). San Francisco, CA: Jossey-Bass.

Clifton, R. A., Perry, R. P., Roberts, L. W., & Peter, T. (2008). Gender, psychological dispositions, and the academic achievement of college students. *Research in Higher Education, 49*, 684–703.

Connolly, M. (2000). Issues for lesbian, gay, and bisexual students in traditional classrooms. In V. A. Wall & N. J. Evans (Eds.), *Toward acceptance: Sexual orientation issues on campus* (pp. 107–130). Lanham, MD: American College Personnel Association.

Crenshaw, K. (1994). Mapping the margins: Intersectionality, identity politics, and violence against women of color. *Stanford Law Review, 43*, 1241–1299.

Cuyjet, M. J., & Associates. (2006). *African American men in college.* San Francisco, CA: Jossey-Bass.

D'Augelli, A. R. (1994). Identity development and sexual orientation: Toward a model of lesbian, gay, and bisexual development. In E. J. Trickett, R. J. Watts, & D. Birman (Eds.), *Human diversity: Perspectives on people in context* (pp. 312–333). San Francisco, CA: Jossey-Bass.

Deutsch, N. L., & Schmertz, B. (2011). "Starting from ground zero": Constraints and experiences of adult women returning to college. *The Review of Higher Education, 34*(3), 477–504.

Duffy, J. O. (2007). Invisibly at risk: Low-income students in a middle- and upper-class world. *About Campus, 12*(2), 18–25.

El-Khawas, E. (2003). The many dimensions of student diversity. In S. R. Komives, D. B. Woodard, Jr., & Associates (Eds.), *Student services: A handbook for the profession* (4th ed., pp. 45–62). San Francisco, CA: Jossey-Bass.

Evans, N. J. (2002). The impact of an LGBT safe zone project on campus climate. *Journal of College Student Development, 43*(4), 522–539.

Evans, N. J., Assadi, J. L., & Herriott, T. K. (2005). Encouraging the development of disability allies. In R. D. Reason, E. M. Broido, T. L. Davis, & N. J. Evans (Eds.), *Developing social justice allies: New directions for student services, No. 110* (pp. 67–79). San Francisco, CA: Jossey-Bass.

Evans, N. J., & Broido, E. M. (1999). Coming out in college residence halls: Negotiation, meaning making, challenges, supports. *Journal of College Student Development, 40,* 658–668.

Evans, N. J., & Economos, K. (2010, Fall). Self-authorship and disability. *Standing Committee for Disability Newsletter.* Washington, DC: ACPA.

Evans, N. J., Forney, D. S., Guido, F. M., Patton, L. D., & Renn, K. A. (2010). *Student development in college: Theory, research, and practice* (2nd ed.). San Francisco, CA: Jossey-Bass.

Forney, D. S. (1994). A profile of student affairs master's students: Characteristics, attitudes, and learning styles. *Journal of College Student Development, 35,* 337–345.

French, S. (2000). Equal opportunities: Yes, please. In M. Adams, W. J. Blumenfeld, R. Castañeda, H. W. Hackmann, M. L. Peters, & X. Zúñiga (Eds.), *Readings for diversity and social justice* (pp. 364–366). New York, NY: Routledge.

Frey, R. (2007, September). *Helping adult learners succeed: Tools for two-year colleges.* Report prepared for the Council for Adult and Experiential Learning, Chicago, IL.

Greene, J. P., & Forster, G. (2003). *Public high school graduation and college readiness rates in the United States* (Education Working Paper No. 3, pp. 1–32). New York, NY: Manhattan Institute for Policy Research.

Guardia, J. R., & Evans, N. J. (2008a). Factors influencing the ethnic identity development of Latino fraternity members at a Hispanic serving institution. *Journal of College Student Development, 49,* 163–181.

Guardia, J. R., & Evans, N. J. (2008b). Student development in tribal colleges and universities. *NASPA Journal, 45*(2), 237–264. Retrieved from http://publications.naspa.org/naspajournal/vol45/iss2/art5

Gunasekera, N., & Friedrich, K. (2009). Creating inclusive science, technology, engineering, and mathematics (STEM) courses. In R. A. R. Gurung & L. R. Prieto (Eds.), *Getting culture: Incorporating diversity across the curriculum* (pp. 161–170). Sterling, VA: Stylus.

Gurin, P., Dey, E. L., Hurtado, S., & Gurin, G. (2004). Diversity and higher education: Theory and impact on educational outcomes. *Harvard Educational Review, 72*(3), 330–366.

Hall, L. M., & Belch, H. A. (2000). Setting the context: Reconsidering the principles of full participation and meaningful access for students with disabilities. In H. A. Belch (Ed.), *Serving students with disabilities: New directions for student services, No. 91* (pp. 5–17). San Francisco, CA: Jossey-Bass.

Hall, R. M., & Sandler, B. R. (1984). *Out of the classroom: A chilly campus climate for women?* Report prepared for the Association of American Colleges, Washington, DC.

Hardin, C. J. (2008). Adult students in higher education: A portrait of transitions. In B. O. Barefoot (Ed.), *The first year and beyond: Rethinking the challenge of collegiate transition: New directions for higher education, No. 144* (pp. 49–55). San Francisco, CA: Jossey-Bass.

Harper, S. R., & Hurtado, S. (2007). Nine themes in campus racial climates and implications for institutional transformation. In S. R. Patton & L. D. Patton (Eds.), *Responding to the realities of race on campus: New directions for student services, No. 120* (pp. 7–24). San Francisco, CA: Jossey-Bass.

Harper, S. R., & Nichols, A. H. (2008). Are they not all the same? Racial heterogeneity among Black male undergraduates. *Journal of College Student Development, 49*(3), 199–214.

Hecht, M. L., Jung, E., & Wadsworth, B. C. (2008). The role of identity gaps, discrimination, and acculturation in international students' educational satisfaction in American classrooms. *Communication Education, 57*(1), 64–87.

Higbee, J. L., & Barajas, H. L. (2007). Building effective places for multicultural learning. *About Campus, 12*(3), 16–22.

Hirt, J. B. (2006). *Where you work matters: Student affairs administration at different types of institutions.* Lanham, MD: University Press of America.

Hurtado, S. (2003). Institutional diversity in American higher education. In S. R. Komives, D. B. Woodard, Jr., & Associates (Eds.), *Student services: A handbook for the profession* (4th ed., pp. 23–44). San Francisco, CA: Jossey-Bass.

Hurtado, S., Milem, J., Clayton-Petersen, A., & Allen, W. (1999). *Enacting diverse learning environments: Improving the climate for racial/ethnic diversity in higher education* (ASHE-ERIC Higher Education Report, Vol. 26, No. 8). Washington, DC: George Washington University, Graduate School of Education and Human Development.

Institute of International Education. (2010). Open doors: Fast facts. Retrieved from www.iie.org/en/Research-and-Publications/Open-Doors

Jehangir, R. R. (2009). Cultivating voice: First-generation students seek full academic citizenship in multicultural learning communities. *Innovative Higher Education, 34*(1), 33–49.

Jehangir, R. R. (2010). *Higher education and first-generation students: Cultivating community, voice, and place for the new majority.* New York, NY: Palgrave Macmillan.

Jones, S. R., & McEwen, M. K. (2000). A conceptual model of multiple dimensions of identity. *Journal of College Student Development, 41,* 405–413.

Kolb, D. A. (1981). Learning styles and disciplinary differences. In A. W. Chickering (Ed.), *The modern American college: Responding to the new realities of diverse students and a changing society* (pp. 232–255). San Francisco, CA: Jossey-Bass.

Mahaffey, C. J., & Smith, S. A. (2009). Creating welcoming campus environments for students from minority religious groups. In S. R. Harper & S. J. Quaye (Eds.), *Student engagement in higher education: Theoretical perspectives and practical approaches for diverse populations* (pp. 80–98). New York, NY: Routledge.

Maple, S. A., & Stage, F. K. (1991). Influences on the choice of math/science major by gender and ethnicity. *American Educational Research Journal, 28*(1), 37–60.

Martinez, M., & Kloppott, S. (2003). Improving access for minority, low-income, and first-generation students. *Pathways to College Network,* 1–15.

Martinez, M., & Kloppott, S. (2005). The link between high school reform and college access and success for low-income and minority youth. *American Youth Policy Forum and Pathways to College Network,* 1–60.

Maxwell, W., & Shammas, D. (2008). Research on race and ethnic relations among community college students. In S. R. Harper (Ed.), *Creating inclusive campus environments for cross-cultural learning and student engagement* (pp. 45–65). Washington, DC: National Association of Student Personnel Administrators.

McBain, L., Kim, Y. M., Cook, B. J., & Snead, K. M. (2012). *From soldier to student II: Assessing campus programs for veterans and service members.* Washington, DC: American Council on Education.

Merisotis, J. P., & O'Brien, C. T. (Eds.). (1998). *Minority-serving institutions: Distinct purposes, common goals: New directions for higher education, No. 102.* San Francisco, CA: Jossey-Bass.

Mitstifer, D. I. (2012). *CAS professional standards for higher education* (8th ed.). Washington, DC: Council for the Advancement of Standards in Higher Education.

Morris, L. K., & Daniel, L. G. (2008). Perceptions of a chilly climate: Differences in traditional and non-traditional majors for women. *Research in Higher Education, 49*(3), 256–273.

Nichols, A. H., & Quaye, S. J. (2009). Beyond accommodation: Removing barriers to academic and social engagement for students with disabilities. In S. R. Harper & S. J. Quaye (Eds.), *Student engagement in higher education* (pp. 39–60). New York, NY: Routledge.

Oldfield, K. (2007). Humble and hopeful: Welcoming first-generation poor and working-class students to college. *About Campus, 11*(6), 2–12.

Ortiz, A. M., & Santos, S. J. (2009). *Ethnicity in college: Advancing theory and improving diversity practices on campus.* Sterling, VA: Stylus.

Ostrove, J. M., & Long, S. M. (2007). Social class and belonging: Implications for college adjustment. *The Review of Higher Education, 30*(4), 363–389.

Pascarella, E. T., Pierson, C. T., Wolniak, G. C., & Terenzini, P. T. (2004). First-generation college students: Additional evidence on college experiences and outcomes. *Journal of Higher Education, 75*(3), 249–284.

Pascarella, E. T., & Terenzini, P. T. (2005). *How college affects students: A third decade of research* (Vol. 2). San Francisco, CA: Jossey-Bass.

Pizzolato, J. E. (2003). Developing self-authorship: Exploring the experiences of high-risk college students. *Journal of College Student Development, 44,* 797–811.

Pliner, S. M., & Johnson, J. R. (2004). Historical, theoretical, and foundational principles of Universal Instructional Design in higher education. *Equity and Excellence in Education, 37*(2), 105–113.

Rayle, A. D., & Chung, K. (2008). Revisiting first-year college students' matter: Social support, academic stress, and the mattering experience. *Journal of College Student Retention: Research, Theory, and Practice, 9*(1), 21–37.

Rendón, L. I. (1994). Validating culturally diverse students: Toward a new model of learning and student development. *Innovative Higher Education, 19,* 33–51.

Renn, K. A. (2004). *Mixed race students in college: The ecology of race, identity, and community on campus.* Albany, NY: University of New York Press.

Rhoads, R. A. (1994). *Coming out in college: The struggle for a queer identity.* Westport, CT: Bergin & Garvey.

Ross-Gordon, J. M. M. (2011). Research on adult learners: Supporting the needs of a student population that is no longer nontraditional. *Peer Review, 13*(1), 1–6.

Rudd, M. D., Goudling, J., & Bryan, C. J. (2011). Student veterans: A national survey exploring psychological symptoms and suicide risk. *Professional Psychology: Research and Practice, 42*(5), 354–360.

Rudolph, F. (1962). *The American college and university: A history.* Athens, GA: University of Georgia Press.

Rumann, C. B., & Hamrick, F. A. (2010). Student veterans in transition: Re-enrolling after war zone deployments. *Journal of Higher Education, 81*(4), 431–458.

Ryan, D. P., & Scura, A. K. (2011, Spring). Disability microaggressions in higher education. *Standing Committee on Disability Newsletter.* Retrieved from www.myacpa.org/sites/default/files/Spring_2011_SCD_Newsletter.pdf

Saddler, T. N. (2010). Mentoring and African American undergraduates' perceptions of academic success. In T. L. Strayhorn & M. C. Terrell (Eds.), *The evolving challenges of Black college students: New insights for policy and practice* (pp. 179–200). Sterling, VA: Stylus.

Sander, L. (2012, March 11). Out of uniform: At half a million and counting, veterans cash in on Post-9/11 GI Bill. *The Chronicle of Higher Education.* Retrieved from http://chronicle.com/article/At-Half-a-Million-and/131112/

Schlossberg, N. K. (1989). Marginality and mattering: Key issues in building community. In D. C. Roberts (Ed.), *Designing campus activities to foster a sense of community: New directions for student services, No. 48* (pp. 5–15). San Francisco, CA: Jossey-Bass.

Seifert, T. (2007). Understanding Christian privilege: Managing the tensions of spiritual plurality. *About Campus, 12*(2), 10–17.

Silver, P., Bourke, A., & Strehorn, K. C. (1998). Universal instructional design in higher education: An approach for inclusion. *Equity and Excellence in Education, 31*(2), 47–51.

Silverman, S. C., Aliabadi, S., & Stiles, M. R. (2009). Meeting the needs of commuter, part-time, transfer, and returning students. In S. R. Harper & S. J. Quaye (Eds.), *Student engagement in higher education* (pp. 223–241). New York, NY: Routledge.

Solórzano, D., Ceja, M., & Yosso, T. (2000). Critical race theory, racial microaggressions, and campus racial climate: The experiences of African American college students. *Journal of Negro Education, 69*(1–2), 60–73.

Sparks, R. L., & Lovett, B. J. (2009). College students with learning disabilities diagnoses. *Journal of Learning Disabilities, 42,* 494–510.

Strayhorn, T. L., Blakewood, A. M., & DeVita, J. M. (2008). Factors affecting the college choice of African American gay male undergraduates: Implications for retention. *NASAP Journal, 11*(1), 88–108.

Strayhorn, T. L., & Terrell, M. C. (Eds.). (2010). *The evolving challenges of Black college students: New insights for policy and practice.* Sterling, VA: Stylus.

Tate, W. (2001). Science education as a civil right: Urban schools and opportunity-to-learn considerations. *Journal of Research in Science Teaching, 38*(9), 1015–1028.

Thelin, J. R. (2004). *A history of American higher education.* Baltimore, MD: Johns Hopkins University Press.

U.S. Department of Education, National Center for Education Statistics. (2011a). Do you have information on postsecondary enrollment rates? *Digest of Education Statistics, 2010* (NCES 2011–015, chap. 3). Retrieved from http://nces.ed.gov/fastfacts/display.asp?id=98

U.S. Department of Education, National Center for Education Statistics. (2011b). How many students in postsecondary education have a disability? *Digest of*

Education Statistics, 2010 (NCES 2011–015, chap. 3). Retrieved from http://nces.ed.gov/fastfacts/display.asp?id=60

Villalpando, O. (2004). Practical considerations of critical race theory and Latino critical theory for Latino college students. In A. M. Ortiz (Ed.), *Addressing the unique needs of Latino American students: New directions for student services, No. 105* (pp. 41–50). San Francisco, CA: Jossey-Bass.

Whiteman, S. D., Barry, A. E., Mroczek, D. K., & Wadsworth, S. M. (2013). The development and implications of peer emotional support for student service members/veterans and civilian college students. *Journal of Counseling Psychology, 60*(2), 265–278.

Yamazaki, Y. (2005). Learning styles and typologies of cultural differences: A theoretical and empirical comparison. *International Journal of Intercultural Relations, 29*, 521–548.

Zemke, R., & Zemke, S. (1995). Adult learning: What do we know for sure? *TRAINING*, 39–50.

Part Two

Theory Into Practice

STUDENT AFFAIRS AS A profession prides itself on putting theory into practice. Practitioners deploy the tenets or underpinning of a theory in actual work with students. This approach allows the field to refine its ideas and to develop other successful methods of enhancing students' learning outcomes. The final three chapters of Student Affairs for Academic Administrators demonstrate how student affairs theories can be put into practice within academic affairs units.

In chapter 4, the elements contributing to successful collaboration between academic affairs and student affairs are explored. In chapter 5, illustrations of academic honor programs where academic and student affairs professionals collaborate and can use student development theory to enhance students' learning outcomes are shared. In chapter 6, student development theory is applied to undergraduate research programs. In this instance, student-affairs-related theories are implemented in an environment that typically resides exclusively within academic affairs, thus giving readers the chance to consider the theories' applicability to educational experiences outside student affairs.

4

Collaboration

Adrianna Kezar

Helen Jones, provost of Hilltop University, had been interested in engaging students more deeply in their learning in their first year and easing their transition to college. A faculty committee had been meeting for over a year, but the recommendations they developed, although showing some promise, seemed as if they might not be forward thinking enough. She worried students would not find them truly engaging. Also, although the committee was informed that recommendations needed to be cost neutral, if not cost cutting, given the decline in state budgets, most of their ideas entailed additional funding. A draft set of recommendations was developed at the year-end meeting, and the faculty made plans to meet in the fall to refine and implement ideas.

Jones did not know exactly what was missing but felt some added expertise was needed. She contacted the vice president for student affairs, Harold Fields; shared the draft recommendations; and asked whether there were staff in student affairs who might have ideas for enhancing students' first-year experience and might join the committee next year during its deliberations. Fields was excited by the request, as his staff had developed several ideas over the years but had been unable to garner support and resources to move them forward. Also, student affairs had already been hit with budget cuts, so their recommendations for change were all cost neutral or had minimal associated costs.

One idea was creating virtual first-year communities through Facebook, where students would meet prior to orientation and stay connected all year whether they lived on campus or commuted. Another notion was a mentor pro-

gram in which the previous year's first-year students would become mentors for the next year's entering class. Yet another concept was a series of service opportunities during students' first year linked to course material: doing environmental projects, helping at a homeless shelter, and working with an education outreach program conducting tutoring. Student affairs staff had wanted to link these to faculty courses and engage faculty but had not found willing faculty.

Jones and Fields decided on four student affairs staff members to join the faculty subcommittee. They contacted the chair of the faculty committee and explained that an interesting opportunity had presented itself: Student affairs had a series of recommendations for learning opportunities, programs, and services that could enhance students' first-year experience, and they hoped that these recommendations could be reviewed and potentially integrated into faculty recommendations. The chair was a bit worried that other faculty might feel this proposal was backtracking from the ideas they had developed, but through further discussion, the chair saw the value of the new ideas and realized that if the expansion was presented carefully to the group, it could be seen as an opportunity.

The faculty chair, Audrey Nelson, asked that she be able to hold the first meeting just with faculty to ensure everyone was comfortable with the new arrangement and to air any concerns prior to the new members joining the session. She sent several e-mails to the committee and obtained agreement, and then they had their first meeting of the year. A few faculty members registered that some of the ideas did not seem academic enough in focus, and Nelson explained that the reasons for the joint meeting were (a) to get faculty to add their ideas to the student affairs recommendations and to have the student affairs staff help modify faculty ideas to be more engaging, (b) to increase use of social media, and (c) to consider out-of-classroom venues and experiential opportunities to expand learning.

Having worked through concerns, the student affairs cohort was invited to the next meeting. At that meeting, Fields was invited to provide an overview of his division and ways it enhanced student learning on campus. He also introduced the four student affairs staff members and described their roles and how they fit into the overall goals of the division. At the next meeting, the complete committee began work again on the recommendations. Everyone agreed that the virtual learning communities had great potential at this commuter campus. The committee worked on ways to integrate faculty and staff into the virtual community and helped link discussion and materials for courses through the learning communities. Although they tackled this issue first, they ended up developing a rich set of recommendations that drew on both of their original recommendations but substantially altered each given their dif-

fering expertise. This committee helped create a new tradition of joint faculty and student affairs committees, which have become more common. Certainly faculty and staff had met before about certain issues, such as advising, but those meetings were seen as more anomalous and not common practice.

LUCKILY FOR STUDENTS, COLLABORATION between academic affairs and student affairs, as described in the opening fictional vignette, is becoming more common. Two decades ago, student and academic affairs work was largely separate on most campuses across the country. Literature has described the enormous gulf between these two divisions that had become separate cultures on campus (Kezar, Hirsch, & Burack, 2002; Knefelkamp, 1991; Kuh, Douglas, Lund, & Ramin-Gyurnek, 1994; Love & Love, 1995). Originally, the gulf was seen as a natural division of labor, reflecting two perceived separate domains of student life, in the classroom and out of the classroom. But research on student learning and experience in the 1980s and 1990s identified how this historic division was not helpful for student learning and, in fact, was preventing a coherent or seamless learning experience (Kuh et al., 1994; Love & Love, 1995).

This chapter addresses several key areas related to creating more collaboration between academic affairs and student affairs professionals. First, the benefits of collaboration are described, providing rationale for engaging in this type of work. Second, some challenges academic affairs administrators might face as they begin to engage in collaboration are noted. Third, key areas where partnerships have been fruitful provide some ideas on where to focus this work are presented. These conjunctions are derived from national studies and an extensive review of research. Fourth, strategies for initiating and sustaining collaborations are reviewed. Although there are enormous benefits to cooperation, many campuses experience difficulty creating shared efforts that work well and are sustained. Fifth, the qualities and characteristics of successful collaborations are examined. Overall, this chapter provides the critical ideas needed for leaders in academic affairs to understand how to move into what might be uncharted waters for their division.

BENEFITS OF STUDENT AFFAIRS AND ACADEMIC AFFAIRS COLLABORATIONS

Although there are a host of documented benefits to collaboration between academic affairs and student affairs, student learning should be the ultimate motivator. Cognitive science, in particular, demonstrates that the application of learning is critical to understanding (Keeling, 2004). Also, the extension of learning into meaningful contexts for students—discussions with peers and experiences outside of the classroom—results in greater learning (Astin, 1993; Chickering & Reisser, 1993; Kuh et al., 1994; Pascarella & Terenzini, 1991). Researchers have described how students have increased opportunities for learning when classroom and out-of-classroom activities are connected experiences building on each other (Knefelkamp, 1991; Kuh et al., 1994; Love & Love, 1995; Schroeder & Hurst, 1996). Recent research by Kuh, Kinzie, Schuh, and Whitt (2005) found that shared responsibility for educational quality and student success is related to stronger levels of student engagement. These authors defined *shared responsibility* as campuses that have active partnerships between student affairs and academic affairs. Although earlier research suggested that collaborations and partnerships would increase student learning, more recent research has found a relationship between the use of partnerships and higher levels of student engagement, a proxy for student learning and development. Although student learning is the primary objective, collaboration also leads to improved graduation rates and enhances retention. For example, research on learning communities—a collaboration between academic affairs and student affairs administration—demonstrates they produce improved learning outcomes and improve retention (Smith & McCann, 2001; Westfall, 1999). Similarly, first-year interest groups help to improve retention (Schroeder, Minor, & Tarkow, 1999).

Research demonstrates many other important benefits resulting from collaborative efforts. In an environment of shrinking resources, one important result of collaborations is the leveraging of resources to offer quality services or programs. For example, if multiple units on a college campus set up separate evaluations of student learning, then costs associated with assessment could be quite high. However, if units work together to assess outcomes, savings might be obtained and resources freed to meet other institutional priorities. In addition, the units and the campus as a whole have a more complex and comprehensive understanding of student learning on that campus.

Organizational learning is another potential outcome resulting from collaborative efforts. Bensimon and Neumann (1993) found that working collaboratively in cross-functional teams develops innovation and learning between units and improves organizational functioning. With tight budgets and need for campus innovation to maintain quality, collaborations that lead to innovative solutions are needed even more. Other researchers (Googins & Rochlin, 2000; Kanter, 1996; Senge, 1990) have demonstrated that bureaucratic and hierarchical organizations reinforce the routine following of policies and procedures. If people are focused on routines and follow policy exclusively, they frequently fail to question ineffective practices and policies or to work innovatively. Conversely, organizations that are set up in a matrix fashion (have both horizontal and vertical linkages among staff), have cross-functional structures (different functions within organizations work together and report to each other), or are team based (units work collaboratively rather than individually and in various functional areas) encourage more interaction, information sharing, communication, and collective problem solving, thus resulting in innovation and learning. In other words, organizations that encourage collaboration have the potential to be more innovative, effective, and efficient.

Another outcome or benefit of campus collaboration is that it creates better service for students in areas such as advising, registration, and career placement (Schroeder, 1999). Although campuses establish individual units to manage a discrete set of activities, processes typically cut across organizational units. In collaborative efforts, where information is shared between offices and communication is open, staff have a better chance of serving students and helping them understand what other office interactions are needed to resolve a particular problem. In addition, these relationships reduce the chance of students being bounced around campus to solve a single matter.

The notion and value of collaboration is not necessarily new to academic affairs administrators. In recent years, interdisciplinary research as a way to solve complex research problems has become well supported across many institutions. Academic leaders can point to national reports such as *Facilitating Interdisciplinary Research* (National Academy of Sciences, Institute of Medicine, & National Academy of Engineering, 2005) as support for collaborative endeavors, which includes research from cognitive science about the benefits of students learning in more seamless ways, as mentioned previously. Similarly, academic leaders such as the late Ernest Boyer of the Carnegie Foundation have called for greater collaboration for enhanced student learning and better campus operations and services. Recent publications and books for academic administrators have challenged the siloed organization of college campuses and advocated for more collaborative forms of work (Ferren & Stanton, 2004).

As academic affairs administrators build on this interest in interdisciplinarity and the challenges of traditionally siloed organizations, they may benefit from key documents focusing on the value of collaboration between academic affairs and student affairs, including *The Student Learning Imperative: Implications for Student Affairs* (American College Personnel Association, 1994), *Powerful Partnerships: A Shared Responsibility for Learning* (American Association for Higher Education, American College Personnel Association, & National Association of Student Personnel Administrators, 1998), and *Learning Reconsidered: A Campus-Wide Focus on the Student Experience* (Keeling, 2004). These documents lend support to the assertion that collaboration between academic affairs and student affairs is needed and provide some ideas and direction for this work.

CHALLENGES THAT ACADEMIC AFFAIRS LEADERS MIGHT FACE

Although the benefits described can be used to bolster arguments for collaboration between academic affairs and student affairs, there are potential barriers that academic leaders should be aware of and plan for. The most systemic challenge is that institutions have been created to support individualistic behaviors, not collaborative ones. Specialization, proliferation of disciplines and departmental structures, narrow faculty training and socialization, individualistic reward systems, bureaucratic and hierarchical administrative structures, differentiation between academic affairs and student affairs, and responsibility-centered budgeting, to name a few, are all structures that developed historically and support individualistic behaviors (Kezar & Lester, 2009). Leaders need to recognize that they may have to restructure these underlying processes to engender collaboration.

Although many faculty members may be familiar with student affairs staff and expertise, it is important for collaboration leaders to provide basic information about programs, services, and roles of student affairs staff and not assume that faculty have an understanding of their work. Without some orientation to the role of those in student affairs, faculty may not see the benefits of collaboration or know how to tap into this expertise. As our fictional faculty chair and vice president for student affairs did within the opening vignette, it helps to create some common ground and understanding about roles. In addition, academic affairs leaders may find their faculty possess unproductive biases or stereotypes of student affairs work as fun and games, unrelated to learning. This is where the documents such as *Powerful Partnerships* (American Association for Higher Education, American College Personnel Association, & National Association of Student Personnel Administrators, 1998) or

Learning Reconsidered (Keeling, 2004) can be extremely helpful by providing examples of how student affairs professionals contribute to campus learning. In addition, highlighting successful partnerships between the two divisions on your campus can help gain support from faculty.

It is important to note that at times both academic affairs and student affairs administrators tend to have slightly different views about how to establish and support collaborations (Kezar, 2003a). In a national survey conducted of academic affairs and student affairs professionals about their views of collaboration between the two groups, student affairs professionals were much more likely to see successful collaboration as an informal process fostered through relationships, whereas leaders in academic affairs tended to want collaborations to be formalized and to restructure operations to support collaborations (Kezar, 2003a). This difference in approach should be discussed and a compromise reached about how much informal work can be completed before restructuring is needed. Student affairs boundaries tend to be more fluid than in academic affairs.

Academic leaders also face the dilemma of having to get faculty to work across different disciplines, and that factor, layered on working cross divisionally, adds another level of challenge (Kezar & Lester, 2009). Faculty across different disciplines often lack similar values and goals, which can complicate efforts to collaborate and develop projects like a learning community or service-learning program. Community and colleagueship are hard to form with so many differences and subcultures represented on committees and working groups. One strategy to address this issue is to choose faculty across disciplines who may have worked together on another initiative to be part of cross-divisional collaborations to reduce the number of new relationships that need to be built. Of course, administrators should be careful not to repeatedly tap only selected faculty so as not to burn them out on collaborative efforts.

Although this section focuses on barriers for academic administrators, it is important to note that student affairs administrators may have their own set of challenges. Faculty is not the only group that may need education. Student affairs professionals may need to be enlightened regarding certain factors within the faculty climate, such as the promotion and tenure structure, before collaborations proceed. In addition, student affairs professionals also bring perspectives and opinions to collaborative efforts. As Cook and Lewis (2007) pointed out, student affairs administrators may have had a negative experience collaborating with academic affairs in the past. It is common to hear about student affairs practitioners feeling treated as second-class citizens in efforts where they were teamed with academic affairs colleagues

(Schroeder, 1999). At points in the history of student affairs, academic affairs staff on some campuses were not helpful partners or were perceived to look down on the profession of student affairs as ancillary and not a primary contributor to the institution or student learning. Both academic affairs and student affairs leaders must note that collaborations are a fresh start and reinforce these new possibilities among their staff and faculty. Ultimately the importance rests on creating shared understanding between the two groups.

AREAS FOR COLLABORATION

Research has demonstrated two key areas for collaborations: programs and problem areas. In terms of programs, studies have demonstrated that beginning with programs or activities where there has been a history of some coordination, such as orientation or first-year programs, can be a very successful strategy (Kezar, 2003a, 2003b; Kezar et al., 2002). Kezar's (2003a, 2003b) national survey found that campuses were most successful with partnerships when they began with an area that already had some coordination of service. The survey also found that areas of coordination differed by institutional type. Community colleges are much more likely to be coordinating on academic advising, whereas faculty at private four-year institutions are working with student affairs on community service-learning. Regardless of the emphasis, common work provides a platform for moving to more and deeper partnerships.

There are a variety of new areas that have shown tremendous promise for collaboration: first-year experience seminars, learning communities, living and learning environments, senior capstone courses, citizenship education, intergroup dialogues, leadership, and social media. Two of these types of programs were highlighted in the opening vignette: first-year programs and learning communities.

On many campuses, first-year experience seminars emerged exclusively in either student affairs or academic affairs. In student affairs, they were often noncredit courses offered as electives and focused on issues such as time management, social involvement, and study skills. First-year seminars that developed in academic affairs not only focused on particular content areas such as understanding human experience and incorporated content from psychology, sociology, and anthropology but also included information relevant to students such as how their own psychosocial development was occurring within the first year of college. More recently, a variety of campuses are recognizing the need for academic affairs and student affairs to partner and offer the experience jointly, thereby using each department's unique expertise. Often courses are team taught by both a student affairs staff member and a faculty member. These courses try to combine goals from both models of first-year experience seminars, such as the purpose of liberal arts education, general education and majors, career exploration, study skills, psychosocial development, and life skills in college such as financial education. *Powerful Partnerships* (American Association for Higher Education, American College Personnel Association, & National Association of Student Personnel Administrators, 1998) provides the example of the College of New Jersey's collaboration between faculty and student life to offer a novel first-year experience program.

Learning communities are another curricular innovation created jointly by student affairs and academic affairs. Learning communities take a variety of forms, but their essential feature is that they intentionally group students together (by matched schedules, living and learning environments, or linked courses with common themes) so that they have the opportunity to work with the same cohort of students over time and, it is hoped, encourage out-of-classroom conversation and engagement. Campuses that partner to offer learning communities often incorporate a residential component. Students enroll in a set of similar courses, and faculty are aware that students live together in the residence halls. Faculty encourage students to extend the conversation into the dining hall or residence hall to create a seamless intellectual experience. In addition, faculty often dine with the students and connect with them outside of class time and in more informal settings. Residential staff become familiar with the content of the courses, offer programming within the residence halls that relate to class topics, and invite faculty to social and programmatic events. A synergy between the learning in and out of the classroom creates an extremely powerful learning experience. The College Park scholars program at the University of Maryland, also described in *Powerful Partnerships* (American Association for Higher Education, American College Personnel Association, & National Association of Student Personnel Administrators, 1998), is an example of a learning community that relies on the expertise of both academic affairs and student affairs.

Problems to be solved are an opportunity for collaboration, particularly those that require broad expertise. Problems requiring broad expertise are increasing retention, achieving general education outcomes, improving graduation rates, responding to institutional accrediting agencies' mandates, fostering civic leadership, and enhancing the success of specific populations

(Hirsch & Burack, 2001). The problems become a common reference point and can help to create a shared vision for undergraduate education or institutional problems (Schroeder, 1999).

Student affairs practitioners are being valued by their academic affairs colleagues for their expertise on the changing student populations and in student retention. Developing cross-campus teams to examine these issues and to jointly develop programs or interventions is becoming an important trend on campuses (Kezar et al., 2002; Schroeder, 1999). Many campuses collect detailed data about students through their institutional research offices, and astute student affairs officers will ask their institutional research offices to develop student profiles and to look at trends and changes in the student body. In addition to using quantitative data, student affairs staff also talk with students and are closely attuned to their experience. Student affairs leaders tend to be well versed in changes within the student body, such as demographic shifts related to race and ethnicity; generational differences; concerns among gay, lesbian, and transgender students; and social and community trends (like helicopter parents of the millennials). These data become extremely valuable for campuses trying to develop programs and interventions for the ever-increasing populations of historically underrepresented students and for meeting the unique and changing needs of students by generation.

Technology has increasingly become important as today's students spend much of their life playing video games, browsing the Internet, or communicating with friends and family. Although technology is a wave of the future, it is also a key area for academic affairs and student affairs to develop partnerships and to work in cross-functional teams. Most campuses are unable to make accurate decisions about technology in ways that can be used to enliven the curriculum and enhance community life unless the expertise of people across campus are drawn on. Student affairs often have staff that are experienced and comfortable with new forms of technology and have experience using them. Technology is also an extremely expensive area where mistakes can be costly. Campus leaders are realizing that cross-functional teams can develop more effective solutions so that resources are not wasted.

WAYS LEADERS CAN SUPPORT COLLABORATION

Not surprisingly, institutional leadership from both academic affairs and student affairs is necessary for ensuring that partnerships are successful (Kezar, 2003a, 2003b). If calls for collaboration are not coming from the top, then faculty and staff members should meet with and garner senior administrative support (usually the chief student affairs and academic affairs officers). Keep in mind that leadership requires not only senior administrative support but also champions who work to nurture and sustain a partnership over the years (Schroeder, 1999). Leaders use several key strategies to garner support: communicating collaboration as a priority, modeling collaboration, capitalizing on external messages, fostering networks, providing resources, creating rewards, hiring new people, and restructuring (Kezar & Lester, 2009).

Leaders can do many simple things to indicate that collaboration is indeed an institutional priority. One of the first ways that leaders can support collaboration is through the values they articulate and how they model collaboration (Kezar & Lester, 2009). As noted earlier, understanding the benefits and communicating them is a strategy academic leaders can use to foster partnerships. However, words alone are not sufficient. Faculty look to academic administrators for some demonstration that collaboration is really a value and contributes to the overall mission and work of the institution. Adding collaboration to division or department mission and values statements, articulating the relationship of collaboration to learning, modeling collaboration in planning and work, and creating dialogues about collaboration are important to student learning, and all reinforce that leaders are serious about staff and faculty working together.

In addition to leaders describing the value of collaboration, they can also use external messages about the need for collaboration to create a sense of urgency and support (Kezar & Lester, 2009). As noted previously, groups such as the National Science Foundation, the National Institutes for Health, disciplinary societies, private foundations, accreditors, and national professional organizations are all communicating the importance of collaboration between academic affairs and student affairs, and campus leaders can use these messages to influence faculty and staff. In short, campuses leaders should become familiar with professional organizations that encourage collaborative work. Campus change agents can determine which external groups have more influence on campus and strategically invoke external messages to garner support for collaborative work.

Collaborations often fail because groups do not undergo the necessary relationship building to create a trusting environment (Kezar & Lester, 2009). Using an existing network that has previously undergone relationship and trust-building exercises offers several advantages. Established networks with knowledgeable and powerful individuals can propel collaborations forward by leveraging knowledge of institutional policies and structures, capitalizing on institutional memory, and connecting people of influence. Networks that have people of influence and knowledge provide the collaboration and capital necessary to move forward quickly and effectively. Furthermore, networks provide the intellectual resources and cognitive complexity needed to overcome barriers that emerge.

Collaborative efforts often involve shifting and, at times, increasing resources. Groups on campus can get only so far if they do not have the appropriate resources to initiate the partnership activities. On many campuses, we hear stories about well-meaning senior administrators who talk about their support for collaboration but do not allocate adequate support when it comes time for the budget process. Leaders need to make sure that the resources are there for partnerships to succeed (Schroeder, 1999). One way to help obtain and sustain resources and support is to examine linkages to the campus mission. Partnerships can be better supported (with human and financial resources) and become a priority if they can be demonstrated to help meet the overall mission.

Senior administrators can also establish rewards and incentives for faculty and staff to engage in partnerships and collaboration (Keeling, 2004). Often the campuses that are successful at collaboration have modified tenure and promotion processes to include involvement in collaborative projects. In addition, bonuses and merit increases are tied to supporting new collaborative initiatives. Last, motivation can also be created through evaluation processes where leaders set expectations about faculty and staff roles and responsibilities inclusive of cooperative efforts. In these meetings, they can stress the importance of the work and help brainstorm ways to be successful.

Leadership also has the ability to hire new faculty and staff (Kezar & Lester, 2009). On many campuses, strategic hires are critical to moving partnerships forward. These new faculty may come from campuses that have already been successful with partnerships or are individuals who have enthusiasm for collaborative work. The experience and energy from new individuals can provide motivation. In general, leaders can reallocate human resources in ways that can provide support for partnerships. As an example, institutional leaders might encourage a faculty member to lead a new learning community rather than serve on a committee.

Furthermore, senior administrators can look for opportunities for restructuring that can better support collaborative endeavors (Keeling, 2004). Many campuses are moving to dual-reporting structures for areas such as orientation, advising, and housing. Others have created joint academic affairs and student affairs divisions so that they are structurally working together on various initiatives. Chief academic affairs officers can also create joint and cross-functional teams to solve institutional problems and issues, as well as work on collaborative programs and projects. Although joint committees are easy to form, leaders are often afraid to restructure units because of the political ramifications—people often resist change in routine, and not making these changes is often easier. But partnerships may end up failing if leaders are not courageous enough to make needed structural changes. Although collaboration can be initiated through these new hires or additional resources, it is sustained when leaders help break down the siloed, individualistic structures and cultures that frequently exist and put in place new processes that support collaborative work. Sustained change means rethinking overall organizational structures, processes, and designs and is described further in the next section of the chapter. (This hard work of redesign is detailed in Kezar and Lester [2009].)

CHARACTERISTICS OF SUCCESSFUL COLLABORATIONS

Although the strategies listed previously constitute many of the characteristics of successful collaborations (having sufficient resources, restructuring, hiring new faculty and staff, creating networks, making collaboration a priority and value, and modeling collaboration), there are additional engagements necessary for sustaining collaboration: (a) seeing collaborations as a developmental process, (b) watching group dynamics, and (c) evaluating (Kezar & Lester, 2009). Although all contribute to long-term success, they are often overlooked. Monitoring them requires a systems approach to thinking about collaboration as an ongoing process.

Seeing Collaborations as a Developmental Process

It is critical for leaders to understand that a collaborative context will not emerge overnight and that they must be visible to guide the campus in the development of a climate supportive of collaborative work. Research of successful academic affairs and student affairs partnerships has identified a development model consisting of the following stages: (a) building commitment, (b) having commitment to action, and (c) sustaining commitment (Kezar & Lester, 2009).

In the first stage, building commitment, leaders motivate people toward a new collaborative approach to work. Change agents talk about the value of collaboration, revise mission and vision statements to speak to collaboration, and create a sense of priority by drawing on external messages that support collaboration. External messages and internal values together help campuses build a story in support of a new way of conducting work.

The second stage, having commitment to action, moves from merely speaking to enacting and supporting collaboration. Senior executives use incentives, hiring, rewards, and modeling to solidify commitment. From altering tenure and promotion standards to creating mini grants and including merit in staff annual reviews, rewards demonstrate priorities and put the stated value of collaboration into practice. Leaders begin changing hiring announcements to reinforce collaboration and hire more people with this perspective.

The third stage, sustaining commitment, requires more formal elements to be put in place. The main elements that emerge for sustaining a context of collaboration on college and university campuses are integrating structure, offering rewards and resources, hiring, and formalizing the network. Sustained collaboration seems highly dependent on redesigning campus systems so the emphasis is on cooperation rather than competition. Campuses may vary in the time it takes for them to go through any particular stage within the model.

Some campuses may have great support for collaboration already; for example, campuses with experience developing learning communities or interdisciplinary research are well set up. These institutions can use this support for one collaborative arrangement to build support for others. Another campus may have had fewer instances of success and need to spend more time in the first stage to build commitment for collaboration. What is important is that leaders gauge where their campus is and not attempt to implement collaboration before initial support or perceived value is there. Also, some leaders forget that once they have implemented collaborations, they need to put structures in place to sustain them. Being aware of stages of development and support assists academic leaders on their journey toward successful collaborative endeavors.

Watching Group Dynamics

Once the collaboration is up and going, leaders' work is not complete; they need to be observant of group dynamics. One of the major areas that can destroy collaborations and partnerships is the formation of dysfunctional group dynamics. Several resources on intergroup dynamics should be given to chairs or facilitators of partnerships to ensure that they have skills in mediating intergroup dynamics and conflict (Bensimon & Neumann, 1993;

Parker, 1990). Attention to intergroup dynamics ensures that communication channels are open, collisions of culture between student affairs and academic affairs are avoided, and personalities are managed. Occasionally, faculty and staff may leave a partnership, and until they are replaced, leaders may need to step in to attend meetings and help the new person transition onto the team. Many partnerships fall apart when key faculty or staff leave and interpersonal dynamics become strained. Trust is low when new people join the group. Leaders need to be aware of these key times and be prepared to step in and be more involved.

Evaluating

Campuses need to make sure that they provide mechanisms to sustain and institutionalize the partnership. One of the key strategies for ensuring partnerships are successful is to evaluate the effort (Schuh, 1999). Evaluation should examine both the process and the outcomes. In terms of the process, questions should examine whether the right people are included, whether there are clear decision-making structures, whether there are appropriate feedback mechanisms and communication channels, whether campuses have the appropriate structure and resources (financial and human), and whether there is a balance in perspective between academic affairs and student affairs. Through these evaluations, leaders and senior administrators have information on which to base decisions regarding resources and direction for continuing the success of the partnership.

Any evaluation should examine student-learning outcomes and whether the learning process appears seamless and benchmark specific goals that have been developed for the partnership. Ultimately, success begets success. Carefully shepherding and then making visible the outcomes of successful partnerships encourage further partnerships.

CONCLUSION

Although partnerships make intuitive sense, higher education institutions are not set up for collaboration. As Philpott and Strange (2003) noted, college campuses in the 1800s were structured for more collaborative work, but changes over the past hundred years have created a situation where "campus constituents may have all but forgotten how to collaborate on common educational goals and programs" (p. 78). This chapter reviewed how campus leaders can overcome historic divisions by being aware of this legacy and potential barriers; capitalizing on key problems and areas of entrée; using strategies that support collaborative work and ensuring characteristics of successful collaboration, seeing it as a developmental process, attending to group dynamics, and conducting evaluation.

REFERENCES

American Association for Higher Education, American College Personnel Association, & National Association of Student Personnel Administrators. (1998). *Powerful partnerships: A shared responsibility for learning.* Washington, DC: Author.

American College Personnel Association. (1994). *The student learning imperative: Implications for student affairs.* Washington, DC: Author.

Astin, A. (1993). *What matters in college?* San Francisco, CA: Jossey-Bass.

Bensimon, E. M., & Neumann, A. (1993). *Redesigning collegiate leadership: Teams and teamwork in higher education.* Baltimore, MD: Johns Hopkins University Press.

Chickering, A., & Reisser, L. (1993). *Education and identity.* San Francisco, CA: Jossey-Bass.

Cook, J., & Lewis, C. (Eds.). (2007). *Student and academic affairs collaboration: The divine comity.* Washington, DC: National Association of Student Personnel Administrators.

Ferren, A. S., & Stanton, W. W. (2004). *Leadership through collaboration: The role of the chief academic officer.* Westport, CT: American Council on Education/Praeger.

Googins, B. K., & Rochlin, S. A. (2000). Creating the partnership society: Understanding the rhetoric and reality of cross-sectoral partnerships. *Business and Society Review, 105*(1), 127–144.

Hirsch, D. J., & Burack, C. (2001). Finding points of contact for collaborative work. *New Directions for Higher Education, 116,* 53–62.

Hirsch, D.J., & Burack, C. (2001). Finding points of contact for collaborative work. In A. Kezar, D. J. Hirsch, & C. Burack (eds.), *Special Issue: Understanding the role of academic and student affairs collaboration in creating a successful learning environment* (pp. 53–62). San Francisco, CA: Jossey-Bass.

Kanter, R. M. (1996). Collaborative advantage: The art of alliances. *Harvard Business Review, 72*(4), 96–108.

Keeling, R. P. (Ed.). (2004). *Learning reconsidered: A campus-wide focus on the student experience.* Washington, DC: National Association of Student Personnel Administrators & American College Personnel Association.

Kezar, A. (2003a). Achieving student success: Strategies for creating partnerships between academic and student affairs. *NASPA Journal, 41*(1), 1–22.

Kezar, A. (2003b). Enhancing innovative partnerships: Creating a change model for academic and student affairs collaboration. *Innovative Higher Education, 28*(2), 137–156.

Kezar, A., Hirsch, D., & Burack, K. (Eds.). (2001). *Understanding the role of academic and student affairs collaboration in creating a successful learning environment: New directions for higher education, No. 116.* San Francisco, CA: Jossey-Bass.

Kezar, A., & Lester, J. (2009). *Organizing for collaboration in higher education: A guide for campus leaders.* San Francisco, CA: Jossey-Bass.

Knefelkamp, L. L. (1991). *The seamless curriculum. CIC Deans Institute: Is this good for our students?* Washington, DC: Council for Independent Colleges.

Kuh, G. D., Douglas, K. B., Lund, J. P., & Ramin-Gyurnek, J. (1994). *Student learning outside the classroom: Transcending artificial boundaries* (ASHE-ERIC Higher Education Report, No. 8). Washington, DC: George Washington University, Graduate School of Education and Human Development.

Kuh, G. D., Kinzie, J., Schuh, J. H., & Whitt, E. J. (2005). *Student success in college: Creating conditions that matter.* San Francisco, CA: Jossey-Bass.

Love, P. G., & Love, A. G. (1995). *Enhancing student learning: Intellectual, social, and emotional integration* (ASHE-ERIC Higher Education Report, No. 4). Washington, DC: George Washington University, Graduate School of Education and Human Development.

National Academy of Sciences, Institute of Medicine, & National Academy of Engineering. (2005). *Facilitating interdisciplinary research.* Washington, DC: National Academies Press.

Parker, G. (1990). *Team players and teamwork.* San Francisco, CA: Jossey-Bass.

Pascarella, E., & Terenzini, P. (1991). *How college affects students.* San Francisco, CA: Jossey-Bass.

Philpott, J. L., & Strange, C. (2003). "On the road to Cambridge": A case study of faculty and student affairs in collaboration. *Journal of Higher Education, 74*(1), 77–95.

Schroeder, C. C. (1999). Collaboration and partnerships. In C. S. Johnson & H. E. Cheatham (Eds.), *Higher education trends for the next century: A research agenda for student success* (pp. 43–52). Washington, DC: American College Personnel Association.

Schroeder, C. C., & Hurst, J. C. (1996). Designing learning environments that integrate curricular and cocurricular experiences. *Journal of College Student Development, 37*, 174–181.

Schroeder, C. C., Minor, F. D., & Tarkow, T. A. (1999). *Learning communities: Partnerships between academic and student affairs.* Greensboro, NC: ERIC Counseling and Student Services.

Schuh, J. H. (1999). Guiding principles for evaluating student and academic affairs partnerships. *New Directions for Student Services, 1999*(87), 85–92.

Senge, P. (1990). *The fifth discipline.* New York, NY: Doubleday.

Smith, B. L., & McCann, J. (Eds.). (2001). *Reinventing ourselves: Interdisciplinary education, collaborative learning and experimentation in higher education.* Bolton, MA: Anker.

Westfall, S. B. (1999). Partnerships to connect in- and out-of-class experiences. In J. H. Schuh & E. J. Whitt (Eds.), *Creating successful partnerships between academic and student affairs* (pp. 51–61). San Francisco, CA: Jossey-Bass.

5

Academic Honor Policies

Jennifer Buchanan

THIS CHAPTER DESCRIBES AN aspect of academic administration that provides a natural confluence between the goals and pursuits of academic affairs and those of student affairs. Pressing issues surrounding academic honesty call for a systematic response that acknowledges the centrality of academic integrity to the mission of a higher education institution. The systems perspective requires that the skill sets of both academic affairs and student affairs administrators be employed. Such a response also maximizes the possibility that efforts actually change the cultures of institutions and have a positive impact on the intellectual and ethical development of students.

A review of the recent literature on academic integrity reveals that no tangible breakthroughs have yet been made in combating academic dishonesty on college and university campuses (McCabe, 2005). In 2005 McCabe reported that the frequency of various cheating behaviors had increased substantially since the first studies published by Bowers in 1964. For example, copying from another's test was reported by 23% of students in 1963 as opposed to 52% in 1996, and unauthorized group work rose from 11% to 49% in the same time period (McCabe & Trevino, 1996). Through his extensive nationwide survey conducted at numerous institutions of all sizes, McCabe confirmed that approximately 51% of college and university students reported some kind of academic misconduct related to written academic work. He also found that four fifths of those who reported cheating on written work did so by using the Internet (McCabe, 2005). Although opinions differ regarding how much the overall prevalence of academic dishonesty has increased (Crown & Spiller, 1998), there is a consensus that, nationally, things are not improving.

Technological advances and increasing digitization of materials used in academic work have increased faculty members' and administrators' anxieties about the prevalence of plagiarism, and assessment in online and hybrid courses poses increasingly vexing issues involving confirming the identity of the test-taker (Harmon, Lambrinos, & Buffolino, 2010). *The Chronicle of Higher Education* (Young, 2010) reported that twice as many students reported cheating on homework than on exams (43% versus 22%) and pointed out that technologies enabling instant communication and collaboration or finding an answer key on the Internet have made this kind of unauthorized group work easy for students. The article also described research conducted by Trevor Harding at California Polytechnic State University at San Luis Obispo, who coined the term *technological detachment phenomenon* (Young, 2010, p. 2). He found that students consistently perceived cheating situations as less serious when technology was used to obtain inappropriate information (Young, 2010). Harmon and colleagues (2010) conducted a study of 20 online courses in which 70% of the instructors reported basing approximately half of the course grade on unproctored exams. Each of these results, along with high-profile cheating scandals such as the one at the University of Central Florida in 2010, in which 200 students were accused of cheating on a midterm (Zaragoza, 2010), helps to fuel academic administrators' fears about control over the classroom.

Working to change attitudes and behaviors related to academic integrity is one of the biggest challenges facing academic administrators today. The quality of learning, the very core of an academic institution of any size, public or private, is dependent on the assumption that students are actually completing the assessments given in a particular course. The credibility of every "learning outcome" or other accountability measure reported to the president, board of trustees, state system, or accrediting agency is affected by each student's choice either to wrestle with the subject matter of the course or to buy a paper online. As academic administrators, our commitment to the process of learning, to the reputations of our institutions, and to our own sense of ethics makes facing this challenge inevitable.

THE CURRENT LANDSCAPE

For years, researchers in the area of academic integrity advocated focusing institutional efforts on either building a student culture of academic integrity through programming and engaging students and others in a dialogue about ethics and integrity (Dalton, 1998) or establishing student honor codes in which students take the lead in reporting and adjudicating cases of academic dishonesty (McCabe, Butterfield, & Trevino, 2003). This latter approach is not feasible for the vast majority of colleges and universities because the effectiveness of a true honor code depends on unique historical and cultural factors (Kidwell, Wozniak, & Laurel, 2003). More recently, authors have emphasized the critical role played by faculty (Buchanan & Beckham, 2006; Gallant & Drinan, 2008; McCabe & Pavela, 2004) in changing the ethos on campus and thus the student behavior in the classroom. It seems natural to assume that faculty members should take an active role in countering current environmental norms.

Historically, it has proved difficult to obtain broad faculty involvement in matters related to academic integrity. There is an allure to faculty in avoiding the confrontations that arise when challenging such cultural norms, especially on research-intensive campuses where faculty have weighty responsibilities outside the realm of teaching.

Many studies have revealed that faculty members, especially in schools without an honor code, avoid following institutional academic integrity policies because they question the effectiveness of such procedures (McCabe, 2005; McCabe et al., 2003). For example, McCabe and Pavela (2004) shared the results of the 2003–2004 Center for Academic Integrity survey, which indicated that 44% of faculty members admitted they did not follow through on at least one cheating incident for a variety of reasons. As an example, Thompson (2006) suggested that some faculty members might perceive a lack of support from administrators resulting from the view of "students as customers" (p. 2444) and the related pressures to keep this special (and litigious) generation of students and their parents happy. Thompson recounted her personal experience with this kind of institutional pressure, saying that the only reason she was able to impose sanctions in a particular case over her chair's objections is that student affairs staff on her campus brought forward a record of the student's academic dishonesty in a past term (Thompson, 2006).

Pavela (2009) described what he thinks is an appropriate faculty and staff response to these types of student and parent sensitivities:

Engaging students in dialogue and discussion about ethical issues can raise complaints that faculty and staff are "judgmental" and "insensitive." What is truly insensitive, however, is the aura of the benign, undifferentiated benevolence which too many educators use in their relations with their students. The latter practice has become a sophisticated art of survival which often enables college and university officials to avoid confrontations and quarrels. Unfortunately, it also fails to help students define the boundaries by which they may shape their character. (p. 6)

Juxtaposed with this faculty reluctance to take up the mantle of systemic change as related to academic integrity is a surprising shift in student expectations. Students have expressed frustration with institutions' efforts to promote integrity. McCabe (2005) reported that these students blame both institutional policies and their faculty members' unwillingness to implement them for their failure to embrace a culture of academic integrity. In their "Ten (Updated) Principles of Academic Integrity," McCabe and Pavela (2004) expressed hope that students in the millennial generation are more apt to support institutional efforts to bolster academic integrity than students in the past. Their first principle exhorts us to "recognize and affirm academic integrity as a core institutional value" (McCabe & Pavela, 2004, p. 12). The hope is that once institutions take a stronger stand in this area, a critical mass of students will embrace their efforts to move toward a more ethical campus culture.

CHANGING THE ENVIRONMENT

Gallant and Drinan (2008) suggested that a broad perspective on academic integrity be adopted by institutions, a view that goes beyond a focus on undergraduate cheating and encompasses concern about the integrity of faculty work and that of graduate students. They wrote that colleges and universities need to reimagine how success is viewed, especially if the uncovering of, and a resultant reduction of, academic dishonesty is to become an institutional priority rather than a liability to avoid. Taking a systems-based organizational-change approach, they argued that for academic integrity to become institutionalized, academic administrators must make a commitment to it that is aligned closely with the overall mission of the institution (whether centered on teaching or teaching and research). In this view, academic administrators must take the lead with issues of academic integrity, with student affairs as a valuable partner in those efforts. Gallant and Drinan (2008) stated,

> While the energy and urgency for change may appear in most instances to come from undergraduate students and student affairs administrators, leadership needs to be seen as coming from faculty and academic administrators if the effort is to be sustained. Academic integrity is too close to the central missions of higher education for the leadership to come from other directions. (p. 37)

As academic administrators accept this challenge to lead their institutions toward an ethos of integrity, it is in their best interest to understand the value added by student affairs professionals on their campuses and to find ways, both in structure and in practice, to make the best of their partnership with them.

STUDENT AFFAIRS CONTRIBUTIONS

As described in chapter 1, student affairs staff are found in a variety of institutions and serve a number of functions on our campuses, yet they are exposed to a fairly consistent set of topics in their graduate preparation programs. They study the history of higher education and the legal and financial aspects of administration, and they gain practical experience in developing programs and services to meet the needs of college students. Because knowledge of student development theory is considered essential in effective student affairs practice (Lovell & Kosten, 2000), most graduate programs emphasize student development theories that delve into the intellectual, emotional, and moral development of young adults.

This type of training equips student affairs professionals to contribute in unique ways to help bolster academic integrity. Their knowledge of moral development theories allows them to investigate the role student disciplinary processes play in ethical development (Jones & Watt, 2001; Mullane, 1999) and to use their theoretical knowledge to inform their practice. For example, Kohlberg (1981) posited that humans' moral development proceeds in a stepwise fashion through six distinct stages, beginning with an orientation toward avoiding punishment through obedience, proceeding through stages involving the primacy of social exchanges and conventions, and eventually focusing on making ethical decisions by reliance on principled action. Student affairs staff members may employ Kohlberg's theory as a lens through which to understand and facilitate students' moral and ethical development. They routinely initiate dialogues with students who breach the academic honor policy in order to stimulate higher level moral reasoning, which is of particular interest to this discussion.

One of the ways this training plays out within the dynamics between faculty and student affairs relates to Pavela's (2009) advice quoted earlier in this chapter, namely, the obligation to shape character. Most academic administrators would admit that they know faculty members are much better equipped to stimulate students intellectually through the depth of their knowledge and exposure to their cutting-edge research than to promote students' moral development by providing support to students while challenging their choice to engage in unethical conduct. There is little doubt that effective faculty members facilitate intellectual development through intense interaction with their discipline's knowledge base. If, however, students' moral development is stunted to the point where cheating or plagiarism takes the place of learning, intellectual development is also retarded. Unless that faculty member is in an area such as social work, counseling, or education, he or she probably does not possess the skill set needed to facilitate further development along intellectual and moral dimensions.

Another asset frequently developed by student affairs training and experience is a basic knowledge of legal issues relevant to higher education, especially issues of how much process is due in student disciplinary matters (Kaplin & Lee, 2006), as well as how to avoid personal and institutional liability. This background can give student affairs professionals more confidence than faculty in dealing with difficult situations arising when a student is facing charges of academic dishonesty and can thus help academic administrators provide faculty members guidance on routine procedural questions without having to overtax the institution's attorney. In addition, student judicial programs typically approach interactions with students through the lens of development instead of discipline (Bostic & Gonzalez, 1999). These professionals understand due process well enough to facilitate the legal requirements while working to promote student growth along moral and ethical vectors (Janosik & Riehl, 2000).

Student affairs administrators also often interact with students in informal settings, giving them knowledge of both the general student culture and the subcultures present. These professionals have chosen to spend their careers interacting with, and designing programs for, students. At institutions of all sizes and types, student affairs professionals make it their business to stay attuned to students' ways of interacting, perceived needs, and general health and well-being. This focus generally leads these practitioners to know more than faculty about students' uses of technology, their motivations, and their more "natural" out-of-class behaviors. The insights gained from this experience, especially when students with serious emotional and behavioral difficulties become engaged with the academic integrity system, can be invaluable to faculty and academic administrators. During what many student affairs staff term *teachable moments,* they sometimes can even help a faculty member understand that a student caught cheating is motivated less by disdain for the class than by panic, resulting in the student's reversion to lower levels of maturity and ethical decision-making. In addition, the hope remains that students learn part of their values through observing ethical behaviors exhibited by role models (i.e., faculty members), and that because of their ability to relate to students, student affairs staff can help students make the most of their interactions with faculty to encourage intellectual and ethical development.

ACADEMIC INTEGRITY AS COLLABORATION

The rest of this chapter focuses on how academic administrators who are tackling the daunting task of changing the culture of integrity at their institutions can forge collaborations with student affairs practitioners to accomplish their goals. In that light, both the structure governing academic integrity violations and the process of working with student affairs is examined.

When analyzing the elements of a campus integrity system, one can focus on both the *rule* itself (also known as a *code* or *policy*) and the organizational structure set up to implement that policy. Academic integrity policies differ in terms of whether academic affairs, student affairs, or student participation receives greater emphasis. Some true honor-code institutions, which usually have student-run honor courts, honor pledges, unproctored examinations, and a single sanction for all offenses, maximize student participation in educational efforts and adjudication of cases (McCabe & Trevino, 1996). However, as Kidwell and colleagues (2003) noted, very few colleges and universities (100 out of the 3,500 institutions existing at that time) actually have true honor codes, and most of them exist in private, Ivy League, or similar institutions.

At the opposite extreme, some institutions simply incorporate expectations regarding academic integrity into their code of student conduct governing nonacademic offenses, placing the responsibility for administering the system squarely on the shoulders of student affairs administrators. In this kind of system, faculty members "pass along" cases of academic dishonesty to their student affairs colleagues.

Purely academic systems are more difficult to identify, although there have been calls for more engagement by faculty and academic administrators (Buchanan & Beckham, 2006; McCabe & Pavela, 2004). Many policies mention roles for both student affairs staff and academic administrators, but rarely do they elaborate on the structure of that relationship. There are intentional choices to be made that affect the collaboration between student affairs and academic affairs, especially if institutional leaders choose to revise the academic integrity policy to initiate dialogue and restructure the process.

For many years, higher education administrators, many of them on the student affairs side of the "house," have turned to the International Center for Academic Integrity (ICAI) (see www.academicintegrity.org/icai/home .php for more information) for guidance about code revision and for help in assessing student, faculty, and teaching-assistant attitudes and behaviors regarding the integrity of academic work. ICAI reports that between 20 and 25 institutions request consultation regarding academic honor code revisions annually (A. Monson, personal communication, 2012).

One product of ICAI's work is the "Model Code of Academic Integrity" (Pavela, 2010). The model code is built on the foundation of the basic due process rights owed to students accused of academic dishonesty, yet at a conceptual level, it integrates the important research findings related to academic integrity and findings from other disciplines that concern themselves with issues of human ethical behavior and development. In that vein, it emphasizes giving students ownership of the system through establishment of a student honor council, uses the power of individual commitment through the use of honor pledges, and gives oversight to academic affairs, with administrative assistance from an "honor council coordinator," a likely role for a student affairs staff member. In the model code, individual faculty members have some low-level decision-making authority in their classes, usually restricted to imposing a "0" on the assignment, and honor councils hear more complex cases with policy oversight by academic affairs and day-to-day guidance from student affairs.

For example, one ICAI-guided revision process that resulted in a modified honor code, which is more suited to large institutions, occurred at my institution. The existing code was academically oriented, with the process overseen by academic affairs (see www.fda.fsu.edu/Academics/Academic-Honor-Policy). The institution had a strong history of academic affairs and student affairs collaboration, and the new policy was written to capitalize on that collaboration. Key elements that structure the collaboration included central coordination of the system and faculty advisement provided by academic affairs, sanctioning discretion given to faculty with first-offense cases, second-offense and egregious cases heard by student–faculty panels, and student advisement and educational programming provided by student affairs.

Since the policy's substantive revision in 2005, practice has shown the value of having these clearly delineated roles for academic affairs and student affairs. Students feel supported through the effective and educational advocacy practiced by the student affairs associate deans, and students are sometimes required to go through more formal experiences like an ethics course designed and facilitated through the dean of students department.

The academic nature of the process is reinforced through academic affairs leadership in the oversight committee and the administration of the system. Faculty members receive advisement through academic affairs, decreasing their defensiveness as they increasingly choose to follow the formal process instead of operate outside the university's guidelines. These structural elements culminate in being able to resolve a case either face-to-face with a student in an informal resolution or in a hearing during which faculty and student panel members reach decisions about outcomes and penalties.

It is recommended that institutions employ a model in which the roles played by student affairs and academic affairs are separate and clearly identified but in which collaboration between the two is required. This kind of system capitalizes on the different strengths and potential contributions brought by the two divisions. Hearkening back to Gallant and Drinan's (2008) assertion that change requires academic affairs to take the lead, academic honor codes should reflect the centrality of academic issues. Of course, the most carefully crafted system designed to promote academic integrity is only as good as its implementation. Thus, it is also worth exploring the process-oriented factors affecting academic affairs–student affairs collaboration as outlined by Kezar in the previous chapter.

FURTHER CONSIDERATIONS

Professionals from either academic affairs or student affairs can also serve as boundary spanners. As defined by Williams (2002) in his study, effective *boundary spanners* are individuals who can permeate the boundaries between two or more subgroups of the organization because of their ability to develop and sustain effective relationships, change others' behavior through influence rather than through traditional authority, enact their roles effectively in the organization, and operate within a complex set of organizational structures (Williams, 2002). This kind of boundary spanning can occur in a university setting when a perceived student affairs person becomes employed on the apparently academic side or vice versa.

Contemporary thinkers understand that one part of an organizational system is embedded in the whole, with events that occur in one part affecting all others (Gallant & Drinan, 2008; Williams, 2002). It follows that collaborations between academic affairs and student affairs become more productive if they occur within the context of other positive interactions between the two. Therefore, the more college or university programs bring academic affairs and student affairs together in meaningful ways, the better. Efforts such as managing student enrollment and retention, orienting students and welcoming them to campuses through convocations, and dealing with students whose behavior is of concern both in and out of the classroom can bring together the same administrators who collaborate within the realm of academic integrity. The cochair model has been successful in enhancing this kind of collaboration and emphasizing the partnership between the two divisions.

On the other hand, once appropriate roles are defined by a code or policy, astute administrators will be wise to respect the boundaries of those roles and play their parts without encroaching on their colleagues' scope of authority. Specifically, academic affairs should rely on student affairs for advice regarding due process requirements and for accurate record keeping, as well as for providing advice, support, and counsel to students. Academic affairs should take full responsibility for faculty education and guidance and never put student affairs staff in the position of having to rebuke faculty for deviating from the institution's policy. It goes without saying that the views of academic affairs should also predominate in the realm of research misconduct, whether it involves graduate students or faculty.

CONCLUSION

Confronting issues of academic integrity, including changing student norms and behaviors, is not an easy task. The good news is that it provides a natural confluence with professionals, that is, student affairs colleagues, who are committed to helping students develop into ethical and responsible citizens.

Establishing clear roles within a solid policy and cooperating broadly in shared areas of concern will promote a productive partnership with student affairs that will help academic administrators accomplish shared goals in many arenas.

REFERENCES

Bostic, D., & Gonzalez, G. (1999). Practices, opinions, knowledge, and recommendations from judicial officers in public higher education. *NASPA Journal, 36*(3), 166–183.

Bowers, W. J. (1964). *Student dishonesty and its control in college.* New York, NY: Bureau of Applied Social Research, Columbia University.

Buchanan, J. N., & Beckham, J. C. (2006). A comprehensive academic honor policy for students: Ensuring due process, promoting academic integrity, and involving faculty. *Journal of College and University Law, 33*(1), 97–120.

Crown, D. F., & Spiller, M. S. (1998). Learning from the literature on collegiate cheating: A review of empirical research. *Journal of Business Ethics, 17,* 683–700.

Dalton, J. C. (1998). Creating a climate for academic integrity. In D. Burnett, L. Rudolph, & K. Clifford (Eds.), *Academic integrity matters* (pp. 1–11). Columbus, OH: National Association of Student Personnel Administrators.

Gallant, T. B., & Drinan, P. (2008). Toward a model of academic integrity institutionalization: Informing practice in postsecondary education. *Canadian Journal of Higher Education, 38*(2), 25–43.

Harmon, O. R., Lambrinos, J., & Buffolino, J. (2010). Assessment design and cheating risk in online instruction. *Online Journal of Distance Learning Administration, 8*(3). Retrieved from www.westga.edu/~distance/ojdla/Fall133/harmon_lambrinos_buffolino133.html

Janosik, S. M., & Riehl, J. (2000). Stakeholder support for flexible due process in campus disciplinary hearings. *NASPA Journal, 37*(2), 444–453.

Jones, C. E., & Watt, J. D. (2001). Moral orientation and psychosocial development: Gender and class-standing differences. *NASPA Journal, 39*(1), 1–13.

Kaplin, W. A., & Lee, B. A. (2006). *The law of higher education: A comprehensive guide to legal implications of administrative decision making* (4th ed.). San Francisco, CA: Jossey-Bass.

Kidwell, L. A., Wozniak, K., & Laurel, J. P. (2003). Student reports and faculty perceptions of academic dishonesty. *Teaching Business Ethics, 7*(3), 205–214.

Kohlberg, L. (1981). *The philosophy of moral development: Moral stages and the idea of justice.* San Francisco, CA: Harper & Row.

Lovell, C. D., & Kosten, L. A. (2000). Skills, knowledge, and personal traits neces-
    sary for success as a student affairs administrator: A meta-analysis of thirty years
    of research. *NASPA Journal, 37*(4), 553–572.

McCabe, D. L. (2005). It takes a village: Academic dishonesty and educational
    opportunity. *Liberal Education, 91*(3), 26–31.

McCabe, D. L., Butterfield, K. D., & Trevino, L. K. (2003). Faculty and academic
    integrity: The influence of current honor codes and past honor code experiences.
    Research in Higher Education, 44(3), 367–385.

McCabe, D. L., & Pavela, G. (2004). Ten (updated) principles of academic integ-
    rity: How faculty can foster student honesty. *Change, 36*(3), 10–15.

McCabe, D. L., & Trevino, L. K. (1996). What we know about cheating in college:
    Longitudinal trends and recent developments. *Change, 28*(1), 28–33.

Mullane, S. P. (1999). Fairness, educational value, and moral development in the
    student disciplinary process. *NASPA Journal, 36*(2), 86–95.

Pavela, G. (2009). Academic integrity/due process: Resolving allegations of academic
    dishonesty: A case study. *ASCA Law and Policy Report*, No. 335 (Section 9.42),
    1–10.

Pavela, G. (2010). Model code of academic integrity: 2010. *ASCA Law and Policy
    Report*, No. 350 (Section 10.11), 1–11.

Thompson, C. C. (2006). Unintended lessons: Plagiarism and the university. *Teach-
    ers College Record, 108*(12), 2439–2449.

Williams, P. (2002). The competent boundary spanner. *Public Administration,
    80*(10), 103–124.

Young, J. R. (2010, March 28). High-tech cheating abounds, and professors bear
    some blame. *The Chronicle of Higher Education, 56*(29). Retrieved from http://
    chronicle.com/article/High-Tech-Cheating-on-Homework/64857/

Zaragoza, L. (2010, November 8). UCF probes cheating scandal involving hundreds.
    Orlando Sentinel. Retrieved from http://articles.orlandosentinel.com/2010-11-
    08/news/os-ucf-cheating-test-20101108_1_apparent-cheating-exam-students

6

Promoting Student Development Through Undergraduate Research and Creative Activities

Korine Steinke Wawrzynski

UNDERGRADUATE RESEARCH HAS A rich and distinguished, yet relatively quiet, history on many college and university campuses. For decades, undergraduate research experiences existed for select students in traditional science disciplines, such as chemistry, physics, and biology (Kinkead, 2012). In recent years, it gained momentum and status as an effective teaching pedagogy in undergraduate education, particularly when it was labeled a high-impact learning practice (Kuh, 2008). Whether through senior theses, capstone projects, or independent research opportunities, undergraduate research affords students the opportunity to delve deeply into a topic for an extended period of time under the guidance of a research mentor. Well-designed undergraduate research and creative activity experiences represent excellent opportunities to engage students more deeply into their academics and promote student development in academic, social, and cognitive spheres. This chapter outlines the basic features of undergraduate research experiences, explains how it can promote student development on multiple levels, and highlights common practices.

UNDERGRADUATE RESEARCH AND *CREATIVE ACTIVITY* DEFINED

Undergraduate research represents a collaborative process between faculty and students that combines elements of teaching and research (Dotterer, 2002). Because research and creative activity vary by academic discipline, they assume multiple forms, ranging from a laboratory-based project to a study of a social behavior to a historical analysis to a creative work, such as a musical composition or sculpture (Kinkead, 2003).

Differences exist regarding a definition of *undergraduate research*. The Council on Undergraduate Research (CUR) defined it as "an inquiry or investigation conducted by an undergraduate student that makes an original intellectual or creative contribution to the discipline" (CUR, 2011, ¶ 3). Others have argued that making an original contribution is not imperative but that engaging in the research process, developing discipline-related cognitive skills, and learning about the culture of an academic discipline are sufficient—these activities introduce students to the concept of research and encourage them to pursue it further (Kremer & Bringle, 1990; Lopatto, 2010; Seymour, Hunger, Laursen, & Deantoni, 2004).

HOW UNDERGRADUATE RESEARCH PROMOTES STUDENT DEVELOPMENT

By engaging in an undergraduate research experience, students can make gains in academic, personal, and cognitive development. Undergraduate research is a transformative learning opportunity (Keeling, 2004) that places students at the center of their learning. Furthermore, it contributes to increased student engagement and retention (Kuh, 2008). Although involvement in high-impact learning opportunities, such as undergraduate research, helped all students to persist in school and complete degrees (Astin, 1993; Kuh, 2008; Nagda, Gregerman, Jonides, von Hippel, & Lerner, 1998), its impact is particularly profound on underrepresented student populations, who demonstrated increased retention rates by engaging in a research experience (Hurtado, Cabrera, Lin, Arellano, & Espinosa, 2009; Nagda et al., 1998). Combined, these factors can make undergraduate research an attractive learning opportunity and pedagogical method that promotes student learning and development in multiple spheres, including those that follow.

Academic Abilities

To highlight the impact of undergraduate research on student academic and personal development, Chickering and Reisser's (1993) framework as outlined in chapter 2 of this text is used. Engaging in a research experience improves students' intellectual competence (Chickering & Reisser, 1993) by developing their requisite knowledge and providing opportunities to analyze, problem solve, and reflect on their work. Through a research experience, students can cultivate and improve a variety of academic skills and abilities including information literacy, design and hypothesis construction, data collection and interpretation skills, and knowledge synthesis (Hunter, Laursen, & Seymour, 2006; Lopatto, 2004, 2010; Seymour et al., 2004). As students learn how to identify, locate, and analyze primary literature, they begin to be able to draw connections from the literature to their research, which deepens proficiency in the subject area. Through this knowledge, they can refine a research agenda and learn to design a valid approach to addressing the question. In data collection, students often encounter barriers to their work, such as failed experiments or results that were not significant, but these experiences begin to illustrate how problems may not always have a clear or "right" answer or how insignificant results can influence the direction of one's research. These types of extended learning opportunities provide students a chance to "dig deeply" into their research and cultivate higher-order thinking skills as they try to make meaning of their work.

Personal Development

In addition to academic skills, engaging in a research experience develops important lifelong abilities that can advance interpersonal competence, promote interdependence, and develop purpose in young adults (Chickering & Reisser, 1993). Interpersonal competence relates to a wide array of skills such as listening, asking questions, providing feedback, engaging meaningfully in dialogues, and working productively in a group (Chickering & Reisser, 1993). Depending on the supervisory style of their mentors, student researchers learn how to clarify their roles in research through asking questions, interacting with others, and receiving constructive feedback from mentors and coworkers. Frequently, students in research teams participate in progress meetings, where they engage in dialogue about results and reflect on how findings affect a project's direction. Through progress meetings, research reports, and presentation opportunities, students improve their written and oral communication skills (Hunter et al., 2006; Lopatto, 2004, 2010; Seymour et al., 2004). They learn how to communicate with colleagues about their progress and should be able to explain to nonexperts their research and its significance. Consistent engagement in these types of activities helps to advance interpersonal competence.

Moving through autonomy toward interdependence involves emotional independence, or the freedom from needing continual reassurance from others; instrumental independence, or the ability to perform work independently; and interdependence, or developing an awareness of one's role and obligation to the larger community (Chickering & Reisser, 1993). As students' abilities to collect, analyze, and synthesize data improve, their confidence as researchers grows (Hunter et al., 2006; Lopatto, 2004; Seymour et al., 2004), which strengthens their work and makes them more productive. As they mature as researchers, they require less instruction regarding procedures and protocol, can be assigned progressively more complex tasks, and can work more independently. They learn to establish schedules and routines to get their work done. The research process also teaches students how to collaborate with others to achieve the desired outcomes, as most research experiences involve an element of teamwork, whether working one-on-one with a faculty mentor or working as part of a research team. In both settings, students learn how to work independently and learn to understand how their work contributes to the overall project.

Developing purpose involves being intentional about one's ability to assess interests, clarify goals, make plans, and work through obstacles in regard to career plans, personal interests, and family obligations (Chickering & Reisser, 1993). Engaging in an undergraduate research experience often provides clarification or confirmation regarding graduate school or career plans (Bauer & Bennett, 2003; Hathaway, Nagda, & Gregerman, 2002; Hunter et al., 2006; Hurtado et al., 2009; Lopatto, 2007). Through their work, students interact with faculty and graduate students (depending on institutional type and size) and begin to learn about the culture and norms, as well as the career expectations, of an academic discipline. Students also gain hands-on learning opportunities where they "test drive" what they could do with a particular academic degree. Although campus career development centers and some academic departments try to address the practical question of "What can I do with a particular major?" it is difficult for many undergraduates (and their parents) to comprehend the transferability of many majors or how knowledge and skills learned can be used in jobs after college. However, in a research experience, students have the opportunity to take classroom knowledge and apply it to real-life settings. They see how they can use their education.

Consider the following sample research projects from undergraduate students in a variety of academic majors:

- A student majoring in plant biology worked to develop a fungal-resistant rootstock that would reduce the loss and decline of tart cherry orchards due to root rot.
- A psychology student examined how young children perceive and learn prosocial behaviors such as sharing, comforting, and helping. Implications from this research may influence how parents and early childhood educators can teach these behaviors to children.
- A student majoring in genomics examined how a defect in the protein actin contributes to progressive hearing loss; implications learned from her research may be applied to age-related hearing loss.
- A student majoring in communications examined the impact of using social media and social networking in organ donor awareness campaigns targeted toward motivating young adults to sign up on the donor registry.
- A student majoring in packaging studied the effectiveness of the Food and Drug Administration's patient medication information leaflet that pharmacies include with prescription drugs in an effort to increase patients' comprehension of how to take medicine properly and their understanding of possible risks and side effects.

These examples illustrate the kinds of work students could engage in with a particular major. Their experiences also demonstrate how research and scholarship can contribute to society and improve the world around them. Chickering and Reisser (1993) observed, "Many college students are all dressed up and do not know where they want to go" (p. 50). An undergraduate research opportunity provides students an experiential learning experience that aids them in affirming or refocusing their career paths and provides direction for what happens after college.

Cognitive Development

Cognitive development is defined as how people view knowledge or how they think and reason. The nature of a well-designed and mentored undergraduate research experience should advance students' cognitive reasoning as they become more involved in their project. As noted by Broido in chapter 2, Perry's (1981) scheme for cognitive development outlines several developmental positions relating to how students view knowledge and authorities. The positions are clustered into key groupings: duality, multiplicity, relativism, and commitment in relativism. The three early stages are the most applicable to an undergraduate research experience and illustrate how engaging in research can help to advance a student's cognitive growth.

At the beginning of their research experiences, students need to expand their understanding of the academic foundation of the chosen subject area. Through reading primary literature and trying to understand how it applies to their research question, students begin to develop their knowledge base. At this point, many students could be described as dualistic learners, because they view knowledge as facts to be learned, dispensed by textbook authors and faculty. Students at this developmental stage do not question who created the knowledge or how they did so. Some students may be at the early positions of multiplicity, where they acknowledge the validity of multiple, diverse opinions. Students in advanced positions of multiplicity may think more critically and work more independently as they discover that knowledge needs to be constructed and experts can be questioned. However, most early undergraduate researchers possess a very dualistic understanding of knowledge.

As students become more familiar with the literature, they begin to analyze it critically, discover existing gaps, and generate new questions on previous research. Through conversations with research mentors, they begin to question the literature and slowly realize that questions—as well as their research—may not have concrete answers. Accordingly, they learn how to design their study or experiment to address the disparity in the research and how to carry out their study. Once data collection is complete, data analysis and interpretation are the two primary activities that can move students to advanced positions of multiplicity and possibly relativism, where they recognize that not all opinions are legitimate, multiple factors and contexts need to be considered, and people can disagree on outcomes and opinions. The key developmental outcomes at this stage are that students realize that knowledge is constructed and that they can play a role in creating it. Students have progressed from merely ingesting literature and taking knowledge at face value to actively engaging in its construction.

Advancement along this cognitive spectrum of knowledge acquisition to knowledge construction contributes to the development of *self-authorship*, or "the ability to collect, interpret, and analyze information and reflect on one's own self-beliefs in order to form judgments" (Baxter Magolda, 1998,

p. 143). The journey of self-authorship documents students in understanding what they value, how they interact and form relationships with others, and how they organize and make meaning of the world around them. Baxter Magolda (2001) wrote, "Educators hope that college graduates will experience a transformation from reliance on authority to complex ways of making meaning in which they are able to integrate multiple perspectives and make informed judgments" (p. 24). For us to help steward this transformation, it is critical that we provide students with learning experiences that make them question how knowledge is created and offer them opportunities to mutually construct knowledge with others and examine their role in the process. Various components of an undergraduate research experience (i.e., reviewing literature, designing research inquiry to address questions, interpreting data, and reflecting on the impact of results) can facilitate the complex thinking and reflection needed to advance students along this cognitive spectrum. Because of the considerable time students devote to their research projects and the interactions and guidance of a research mentor, an undergraduate research experience affords students a powerful, extended, complex learning experience compared to what they encounter in daily classroom interactions.

The numerous benefits students receive by engaging in a guided research experience are affected by the complexity and duration of their experiences (Lopatto, 2010). Students who engaged in projects for longer periods of time exhibited greater gains. For example, students who worked on research projects for two consecutive summers were better able to locate and understand primary literature, had more publication and presentation opportunities, reported a greater sense of accomplishment, and gained more leadership experience (Lopatto, 2010).

KEY ELEMENTS OF UNDERGRADUATE RESEARCH AND CREATIVE ACTIVITIES

Although the focus and scope of an undergraduate student's research experience varies widely, effective and meaningful opportunities frequently exhibit several common characteristics. Faculty and administrators interested in initiating an undergraduate research and creative activity program should consider the availability and training of research mentors, the general structure or approach to the research experience, the qualifications of students and any remuneration they may receive, and the program timing and duration.

Research Mentor

The most important component is the participation of a research mentor, often a faculty member or graduate student, who provides structure and feedback (Handelsman, Pfund, Lauffer, & Pribbenow, 2005; Hu, Scheuch, Schwartz, Gaston Gayles, & Li, 2008; Kinkead, 2003; Lopatto, 2004). Some research experiences, often in the humanities and social sciences, center on the student working individually with the faculty member. In the sciences and engineering, research experiences frequently occur in laboratory-based teams, often with other undergraduate students, graduate students, or postdoctoral students. The supervisory and work styles of the research mentor affect the structure of an undergraduate research experience. Lopatto (2010) surveyed student researchers to characterize how their mentors interacted with them and reported five distinct approaches:

- *Learn by example:* The mentor demonstrated how to do the work, and students completed it.
- *Self-organized:* Students completed work on their own.
- *Executive:* The mentor provided written or oral instructions, and students executed the tasks.
- *Division of labor:* The mentor and students divided tasks and worked on them at the same time.
- *Collaboration:* The mentor and students worked together. (p. 26)

Although the nature of the research may influence how and where the data are collected, the mentor establishes the tone for how work is completed and evaluated. Finally, the time a mentor can devote to students affects their perceptions of their research experience and ultimately their productivity.

Faculty should consider how they intend to instruct, supervise, and provide feedback to their student researchers. Resources such as Handelsman's and colleagues' (2005) *Entering Mentoring* or Merkel's and Baker's (2002) *How to Mentor Undergraduate Researchers* can provide guidance regarding the structure of research experiences, effective communication strategies, goal setting, conflict management, and evaluation techniques. Regardless of the format, having students meet with a mentor to guide, discuss, and process their work is a critical component of an undergraduate research opportunity.

Structure of Research Experience

The nature of the academic discipline affects how research is conducted and how data are collected, which influences the structure of the work environment and the tasks assigned to students. For example, some research environments are tightly organized, with a laboratory representing the center of action, where data collection and analysis occur, and researchers with a variety of skills and abilities work together. Other research environments, many that require fieldwork, are loosely structured, with researchers bringing samples back from the field and analyzing them on shared equipment. Still other researchers conduct interviews and transcribe data, but the analysis and consultation with the faculty member are done on an individualized basis (Feldman, Divoll, & Rogan-Klyve, 2009). Research mentors should consider where students fit best into their research setting, where they will be the most productive, and where they have the best potential for growth.

Students' productivity should be evaluated by the nature of the tasks assigned. The goal of many undergraduate research opportunities is to expose students to, and involve them in, the complete spectrum of the research process, which includes locating and reading the primary literature, contributing to the design of the project, training to use equipment and the appropriate techniques or skills to collect data, being involved in data collection and analysis, and creating a written or oral final product (Handelsman et al., 2005; Hu et al., 2008; Kinkead, 2003; Lopatto, 2004). Lopatto (2010) also advocated for having an opportunity to attend a professional meeting or conference and for students to earn credit or pay for their work on the project. Students' degree of engagement in these various tasks varies by their knowledge and ability, previous experience, year in school, and time they can devote to the research. Research mentors should be mindful of these factors as they integrate students into their work environment.

Student Qualifications

Another factor to consider is students' qualifications. Lopatto (2010) noted that grades may not be the best indicators of student performances, as students with average grades often thrive in a laboratory setting. In addition, students' past experiences and talents may influence their training ability, as academically talented students may learn more quickly and require less training than other students. Year in school may also affect their ability to engage in a project. Although junior- or senior-level students will have completed more advanced course work, they may be able to participate in a research project for only a few semesters and not be involved with data analysis or writing. Younger students, who may possess fewer skills and lack the necessary requisite knowledge, can be engaged for a longer period overall, be given greater responsibilities as their skills and knowledge increase, and become active contributors to the research effort in time. These factors vary by the type of project and the preference of the research mentor.

Remuneration

Most students receive some kind of remuneration for their research experiences. Some earn academic credit if the research experience is part of a class requirement or is taken as an independent study, whereas others receive a stipend for their work. As an increasing number of college students need employment to finance their education, it may be advantageous for them to find positions that keep them on campus while providing training and skills that are beneficial for graduate studies or postcollege employment opportunities.

Program Timing and Duration

Undergraduate research experiences can occur during the academic year or over the summer. Benefits and advantages exist for both models. Because faculty continuously work on research throughout the academic year, having students engaged during the fall and spring academic terms makes sense. However, scheduling conflicts may be more prevalent as students are taking courses.

Summer research programs (e.g., National Science Foundation Research Experience for Undergraduates) are shorter and more condensed, often lasting around 10 weeks. Their advantages, however, are numerous, as students often are not taking classes and can spend upwards of 40 hours each week working on their project. Faculty frequently are not teaching during the summer, so they can devote more time to research and mentoring students. Some students take advantage of both models and work on a research project at their home institution during the academic year and work at another university in an intensive summer research program during the summer. Both models provide effective and meaningful research experiences.

When we look beyond the academic discipline, we see these elements comprise the basic components of a typical research experience for undergraduate students. Considering these components can contribute to a better structured and more meaningful research experience.

COMMON PRACTICES IN UNDERGRADUATE RESEARCH

As the nature and practice of research and creative activity vary by discipline, the opportunities and practices within undergraduate research differ by program and institution. Senior-level administrative and widespread faculty support is essential in starting and maintaining an undergraduate research initiative. Upper administration can provide financial support; promote the program among faculty, deans, and other administrators; encourage collaboration between departments; and champion the effort to external constituents. Faculty can consider working with an undergraduate researcher, encourage students to engage in a research or creative experience, and attend campus research events to support their student researchers. Beyond this support, many undergraduate research programs have common features that define their research program. Although the scale of these features depends on institutional type, size, and funding, they enhance the research and creative activity experiences for undergraduates.

Annual Research Forum

Many institutions host an annual research forum or celebration day to showcase the work and accomplishments of undergraduate scholars. Students usually present research via oral presentations or research posters. Fine and performing arts students may give a performance or display creative works. Students receive numerous benefits from participating in a research forum. First, the preparation of their materials (i.e., oral, poster, or performance presentation) requires them to think critically about their project and how to share results or a final product in a meaningful way that meets the guidelines for their particular method of delivery. For example, figuring out how to discuss a yearlong research project during a 10-minute presentation or how to visually display the results of a study on a poster can be challenging. Second, having the opportunity to discuss research results with both experts and nonexperts is a good exercise for students in content comprehension and communication. Third, receiving feedback from visitors—particularly from faculty and graduate students in their respective disciplines—provides an added source of learning, as students engage in dialogue about their work, field questions about methodology and results, and reflect on what they have gained. Under-graduate students are excited about their work, and it is rewarding to watch them engage in conversations and discuss what they have learned.

A research forum also benefits the institution, as it offers a unique oppor-tunity to bring together faculty and students from a multitude of academic disciplines and to exhibit a broad cross section of scholarship and creative activity. It may be the only time philosophy, engineering, social work, music, chemistry, and communication students and faculty are together in one place discussing their scholarly work. Hosting an annual research and arts forum is an excellent approach to promoting an undergraduate research program and showcasing the impressive work of student scholars and their research mentors.

Undergraduate Research Grants

Many institutions provide funding to support and encourage undergraduate research projects. Application procedures vary by institution. The process typically is student or faculty driven. For student-driven grants, students write proposals and find faculty members willing to work with them if funded. The research is sometimes original but more often is related to a faculty member's existing research. In another approach, faculty apply for funding through a dean or central committee, usually by submitting a brief proposal. Faculty then find students to work with them on their particular project. Both approaches are effective.

Benefits and drawbacks exist with both approaches. The student-driven approach places the central responsibility on the students and encourages them to be proactive in seeking mentoring relationships and develop-ing a research proposal. Keep in mind, this approach seems to favor more advanced student researchers, who have more experience, and may exclude younger students, such as first- or second-year students, who have not taken advanced courses or developed research skills, may not be familiar with many faculty, or may not be aware of undergraduate research as a learning oppor-tunity. The faculty-driven approach may increase the number of younger students engaging in research, but it does not help them learn how to find a research opportunity, write a proposal, or initiate conversations with poten-tial research mentors.

The University of Nebraska–Lincoln's Undergraduate Creative Activi-ties and Research Experience (UCARE) program is a combination of both approaches and provides funding for two years. During the first year, students work as research assistants for faculty members on their ongoing scholarship, assisting with research projects, or working in a studio while developing appropriate techniques for their respective fields. In the second year, students advance to more independent projects that they propose and faculty members sponsor. With UCARE, students submit an online applications indicating for whom they will be a research assistant and the project with which they will be assisting. Their faculty mentors receive notification to complete the remainder of the application, highlighting the students' role in the project, explaining how working on the project prepares students for their second year of independent work, and rating the students' ability to carry out the work. This approach fosters shared responsibility between students and their potential research mentors, as students need to find faculty and discuss the possibility of assisting with research, but the faculty member plays an integral role in the preparation of the students.

The University of Michigan–Ann Arbor's Undergraduate Research Opportunity Program (UROP) takes a different approach by helping first- and second-year students facilitate partnerships with faculty and research scientists. Once admitted into the UROP program, students meet regularly with an assigned peer adviser, attend biweekly seminars, and work with the program staff to find a research project that meets their needs and interests. The distinct advantage of UROP is that it engages students in research very early in their collegiate careers.

Finally, many students find research positions by talking with faculty members with whom they have taken a class or who are known to work with undergraduate students. To aid in this process, several institutions post available research positions. The University of Missouri, for example, lists current research jobs on its website, and Michigan State University has Venture, an online database of research, scholarship, and creative opportunities for undergraduates. Some faculty prefer to select students with whom they are familiar, such as students they have had in class or whom colleagues recommend. Therefore, teaching or guiding students on how to approach faculty and share their interests is an additional element to consider when helping to connect students to research opportunities.

Travel Funding

In addition to funding student research, many institutions offer travel grants for undergraduate students who are presenting their scholarship at regional, national, and international meetings. Participating in professional conferences proffers numerous benefits to undergraduate scholars. Presenting research enhances students' communication abilities as they prepare their research or poster presentation and practice their delivery, learn how to answer questions, receive feedback from conference participants, meet professionals in related academic disciplines, and are exposed to other research areas. Typically, institutions offer grants from $500 to $1,000 to contribute toward conference costs.

Having faculty and their undergraduate researchers present their work at meetings can also be a useful recruiting tool for both undergraduate institutions and graduate programs. Undergraduate programs and institutions can develop reputations for being good "feeder programs," or programs where undergraduate students receive strong academic preparation and research experiences that can make students attractive candidates for graduate study. In addition, presenting the work of faculty and students (both graduate and undergraduate students) advances the research reputation of faculty and institutions.

Research Seminars

An undergraduate research experience can be structured as a one-on-one opportunity between a research mentor and a student, or it could be a group experience in a laboratory or research team. Some institutions offer research seminars where students learn about research and engage in a semester-long or yearlong research project as a class. The Honors College at Michigan State University offers research seminars that are course-based research opportunities for first- and second-year students. Students in these small seminars (usually up to 15 students) work with one or two faculty members on a research project from start to completion, with the goal of presenting at the university's annual research and arts forum in the spring. The unique feature of the program is that the entire class works together on the research project as students learn about data collection, research ethics and conduct, data analysis, and preparing results for dissemination.

Another unique approach to a research seminar is the Program for Undergraduate Research in the Life-Sciences (PURL) at Michigan State University. In PURL, students participate in informal seminars designed to help them figure out what research is and if they are interested in engaging in it. Students engage in discussion, take field trips to different research facilities around the state of Michigan, and meet researchers to learn about what they do. At the end of the introductory seminar, students can apply for a one-year lab rotation through four different laboratories during their sophomore year. These seminar formats provide different approaches to undergraduate research that can engage larger groups of students in a research experience, thereby affecting great numbers of students.

Research Contracts and Program Guides

Navigating an undergraduate research experience can be challenging to students and their research advisers. Some institutions have created program guidebooks and contracts to outline program expectations and to increase awareness regarding resources. For example, Utah State University's *Research Fellows Guidebook* explains the various research opportunities available through each college, provides a timeline of goals organized by a student's year in school, outlines the roles of various campus offices and responsibilities of the research fellow, and reviews logistical components to their research program (i.e., compensation, time commitment, academic credit, responsible conduct of research, letters of recommendation). Other institutions have created contracts or letters of intent that help the research mentor and student articulate the student's research goals, the student's role in a project, and faculty expectations. These types of documents provide a general scaffolding that can aid in providing an effective and meaningful research experience.

Undergraduate Research Journals

There are several peer-reviewed undergraduate research journals that are devoted to publishing the works of undergraduate students. Similar to professional journals, some are discipline specific (i.e., *Journal of Undergraduate Chemistry Research* or *History Matters*), whereas others are interdisciplinary (i.e., *The Honors Review, Auctus, Reinvention*). Some institutions also sponsor their own undergraduate research journal exclusively for their undergraduate student researchers (i.e., *Explorations, The Texas A&M Undergraduate Journal, Elon Journal of Undergraduate Research in Communications, ReCUR: Red Cedar Undergraduate Research*). Although having an undergraduate research journal is not a required feature of an undergraduate research program, it does provide an additional venue to promote student scholarship to both internal and external audiences and can be used as a fund-raising tool with alumni and donors.

Undergraduate research opportunities and programs share several common features. Special attention should focus on increasing students' awareness about undergraduate research as a learning opportunity, the structure and logistics of the experience, and the opportunity to share their research. Collectively, these experiences provide engaging and high-impact learning experiences for students.

CONCLUSION

There are multiple approaches to promoting student development through the collegiate years. Undergraduate research is uniquely positioned because it combines research and teaching in a hands-on, applied learning experience. The inquiry-based pedagogy improves a host of academic, social, and cognitive skills and abilities that are integral not only for personal success but also for achievement and advancement in the workplace, graduate studies, and communities beyond academia. Academic administrators in higher education can advocate for the development and institutionalization of high-impact learning opportunities, like undergraduate research and creative activity, to improve student learning, development, and retention.

REFERENCES

Astin, A. W. (1993). *What matters in college? Four critical years revisited.* San Francisco, CA: Jossey-Bass.

Bauer, K. W., & Bennett, J. S. (2003). Alumni perceptions used to assess undergraduate research experience. *Journal of Higher Education, 74*(2), 210–230.

Baxter Magolda, M. B. (1998). Developing self-authorship in young adult life. *Journal of College Student Development, 39*(2), 143–156.

Baxter Magolda, M. B. (2001). *Making their own way: Narratives for transforming higher education to promote self-development.* Sterling, VA: Stylus.

Chickering, A. W., & Reisser, L. (1993). *Education and identity* (2nd ed.). San Francisco, CA: Jossey-Bass.

Council on Undergraduate Research. (2011). About the Council on Undergraduate Research. Retrieved from www.cur.org/about.html

Dotterer, R. L. (2002). Student-faculty collaborations, undergraduate research, and collaboration as an administrative model. In K. Zahorski (Ed.), *Scholarship in the postmodern era: New venues, new values, new visions. New directions for teaching and learning, No. 90* (pp. 81–89). San Francisco, CA: Jossey-Bass.

Feldman, A., Divoll, K., & Rogan-Klyve, A. (2009). Research education of new scientists: Implications for science teacher education. *Journal of Research in Science Teaching, 46*(4), 442–459.

Handelsman, J., Pfund, C., Lauffer, S. M., & Pribbenow, C. M. (2005). *Entering mentoring.* Madison, WI: The Wisconsin Program for Scientific Teaching. Retrieved from www.hhmi.org/resources/labmanagement/downloads/entering_mentoring.pdf

Hathaway, R. S., Nagda, B. A., & Gregerman, S. R. (2002). The relationship of undergraduate research participation to graduate and professional education pursuit: An empirical study. *Journal of College Student Development, 43*(5), 614–631.

Hu, S., Scheuch, K., Schwartz, R. A., Gaston Gayles, J., & Li, S. (2008). *Reinventing undergraduate education: Engaging college students in research and creative activities* (ASHE Higher Education Report, Vol. 33, No. 4). Hoboken, NJ: Wiley Periodicals.

Hunter, A. B., Laursen, S. L., & Seymour, E. (2006). Becoming a scientist: The role of undergraduate research in students' cognitive, personal, and professional development. *Science Education, 91*(10), 36–74.

Hurtado, S., Cabrera, N. L., Lin, M. H., Arellano, L., & Espinosa, L. L. (2009). Diversifying science: Underrepresented student experiences in structured research programs. *Research in Higher Education, 50*(2), 189–214.

Keeling, R. P. (Ed.). (2004). *Learning reconsidered: A campus-wide focus on the student experience.* Washington, DC: National Association of Student Personnel Administrators and the American College Personnel Association.

Kinkead, J. (2003). Learning through inquiry: An overview of undergraduate research. In J. Kinkead (Ed.), *Valuing and supporting undergraduate research: New directions for teaching and learning, No. 93* (pp. 5–17). San Francisco, CA: Jossey-Bass.

Kinkead, J. (2012, June). *What's in a name? A brief history of undergraduate research.* Paper presented at the Council on Undergraduate Research Annual Meeting, Ewing, NJ.

Kremer, J. F., & Bringle, R. G. (1990). The effects of an intensive research experience on the careers of talented undergraduates. *Journal of Research and Development in Education, 24*(1), 1–5.

Kuh, G. D. (2008). *High-impact educational practices: What they are, who has access to them, and why they matter.* Washington, DC: Association of American Colleges and Universities.

Lopatto, D. (2004). Survey of undergraduate research experiences (SURE): First findings. *Cell Biology Education, 3*(4), 270–277.

Lopatto, D. (2007). Undergraduate research experiences support science career decisions and active learning. *Life Sciences Education, 6*(4), 297–306.

Lopatto, D. (2010). *Science in solution: The impact of undergraduate research on student learning.* Washington, DC: Council on Undergraduate Research and Research Corporation for Science Advancement.

Merkel, C. A., & Baker, S. M. (2002). *How to mentor undergraduate researchers.* Washington, DC: Council on Undergraduate Research.

Nagda, B. A., Gregerman, S. R., Jonides, J., von Hippel, W. J., & Lerner, J. S. (1998). Undergraduate student-faculty research partnerships affect student retention. *Review of Higher Education, 22*(1), 55–72.

Perry, W. G. (1981). Cognitive and ethical growth: The making of meaning. In A. W. Chickering & Associates (Eds.), *The modern American college* (pp. 76–116). San Francisco, CA: Jossey-Bass.

Seymour, E., Hunger, A. B., Laursen, S., & Deantoni, T. (2004). *Establishing the benefits of research experiences for undergraduates in the sciences: First findings from a three-year study.* Boulder, CO: Center to Advance Research and Teaching in the Social Sciences.

About the Contributors

HOLLEY A. BELCH is a professor in the student affairs in higher education department at Indiana University of Pennsylvania. She earned a doctorate in 1991 and a master's degree in 1981 from Bowling Green State University. She has worked in a variety of student affairs positions in residence life, orientation, and student activities; as associate dean of students; and as coordinator of research and evaluation for student affairs. The focus of her research includes examining the experience of students with psychological disabilities and the experience and preparedness of student affairs professionals working with this subpopulation. She has published work in the *Journal of College Student Retention*, *Journal of College Student Development*, the *NASPA Journal*, NASPA Monograph series, and in three distinct *New Directions for Student Services* series books. She has served the professional community as an invited lecturer, consulted with a variety of institutions, and presented her research numerous times at national conferences.

ELLEN M. BROIDO is an associate professor of higher education and student affairs at Bowling Green State University, where she has worked since 2001. She also serves as an affiliated faculty member in the Women, Gender, and Sexuality Studies program. She received her bachelor of arts in biology from Columbia College of Columbia University (1987), her master of science in education in higher education and student affairs and in counseling and guidance from Indiana University (1990), and her doctorate of education in counselor education from the Pennsylvania State University (1997). Prior to her work at Bowling Green State University, she served as coordinator of university studies–student affairs partnerships at Portland State University, as well as an assistant professor of university studies (1997–2001), and worked in the residence life program at the University of Massachusetts at Amherst (1990–1994).

Broido's research focuses on social justice issues on college campuses and the experiences of underrepresented or marginalized groups in higher education, with particular attention to disability and gender issues in higher education, the development and effects of undergraduate students' social identities on their collegiate experiences, and the effects of the environment on students from targeted social groups.

Broido's publications include *Disability in Higher Education: A Social Justice Approach* (coauthored with Nancy Evans, Kirsten Brown, and Autumn Watts; Jossey-Bass, in press) and *Developing Social Justice Allies* (coedited with Robert Reason, Nancy Evans, and Tracy Davis; Jossey-Bass, 2005). In addition, she has authored or coauthored 18 book chapters and 12 journal articles. Broido has served on the governing board of ACPA: College Student Educators International, as the editor of ACPA's Books and Media board, and on the editorial review board of the *Journal of College Student Development*.

JENNIFER BUCHANAN is the associate vice president for faculty development and advancement at Florida State University. She spearheaded efforts to revise the honor policy in 2005 and 2010. In 2006 she published an article in the *Journal of College and University Law* with Dr. Joe Beckham titled "A Comprehensive Academic Honor Policy for Students: Ensuring Due Process, Promoting Academic Integrity, and Involving Faculty" (Vol. 33, No. 1). Her responsibilities include supervising staff members and coordinating faculty development processes such as promotion, tenure, and sabbaticals, as well as the academic honor policy and professional development; interpreting and communicating academic policies; resolving student academic grievances; working with academic units to develop degree programs, majors, and certificate programs; helping to design educational programs for deans and department chairs; and responding to requests from governing boards. She also cochairs the Student Situation Resolution Team, which deals with difficult student situations. Before joining Florida State University's Dean of the Faculties Office in 2004, she served as an associate dean in the College of Communication. Prior to that, she held various positions in student affairs, including assistant dean of students and associate dean of students. Buchanan earned her BA in psychology from the University of North Carolina at Chapel Hill (1980), her MA in student personnel work from the Ohio State University (1982), and her PhD in communication theory and research from Florida State University (1998).

JAMES DEVITA is an assistant professor of higher education at the University of North Carolina Wilmington (UNCW). DeVita earned his doctorate in higher education administration from the University of Tennessee in Knoxville, where his dissertation included three research projects on the experiences and development of gay male college students. He currently works with the Applied Learning and Teaching Community (ALTC) as an associate fellow and serves as the program coordinator for the higher education concentration in the master of education program at UNCW. He also serves as the lead evaluator for a $1.4 million state department grant awarded to a group of UNCW faculty in November 2015. He has presented at numerous international conferences, including Association for the Study of Higher Education (ASHE), American Educational Research Association (AERA), and ACPA: College Student Educators International, and published in journals such as the *Journal of Student Affairs Research and Practice*. He currently teaches both master's- and doctoral-level courses that focus on student learning and development, social justice topics in education, and research methods. His research examines the experiences of targeted populations in higher education, particularly lesbian, gay, bisexual, and transgender students and racial and ethnic minorities, as well as scholarship on teaching and learning that integrates applied and online learning.

NANCY J. EVANS holds degrees from the State University of New York, College at Potsdam in social science; Southern Illinois University in higher education–college student personnel; University of Missouri–Columbia in counseling psychology; and Western Illinois University in theater directing. She began her career in higher education in 1972, serving 8 years as a student affairs professional and 33 years as a faculty member, the past 16 years at Iowa State University. She retired from her faculty position at Iowa State in 2013. She is currently using her theater training, serving as dramaturge for the StageWest Theatre Company of Des Moines, Iowa.

During her career, Evans advised 182 master's and 32 PhD degree recipients. She has taught a wide range of courses in the student affairs curriculum, most recently student development theory, social identity theory, campus environments and cultures, and the master's capstone seminar.

Evans has contributed extensively to the professional literature and is best known as the author of two editions of *Student Development in College: Theory, Research, and Practice* (Jossey-Bass, 2009), as well as two books on the experiences of lesbian, gay, bisexual, and transgender (LGBT) students in college: *Beyond Tolerance: Gays, Lesbians and Bisexuals on Campus* (coedited with Vernon Wall;

University Press of America/American College Personnel Association, 1992) and *Toward Acceptance: Sexual Orientation Issues on Campus* (coedited with Vernon Wall; University Press of America/American College Personnel Association, 1999). She is currently completing a book titled *Disability in Higher Education: A Social Justice Approach* (coedited with Ellen Broido, Kirsten R. Brown, and Autumn Wilke Jossey-Bass, 2016). Her research has focused on the impact of the campus environment on members of minoritized populations, particularly LGBT students and students with disabilities.

Evans has been actively involved in professional student affairs organizations, especially ACPA: College Student Educators International, serving as its president in 2001–2002, and has received numerous professional awards from ACPA, including Voice of Inclusion, Senior Scholar, and Contribution to Knowledge. In 2015, she received ACPA's Lifetime Achievement Award.

JEANNE GUNNER, now retired, is a former vice chancellor and English professor at Chapman University. She completed her PhD in comparative literature at Rutgers University and was a faculty member at the University of California, Los Angeles and Santa Clara University.

T. LYNN HOGAN is director of critical thinking initiatives at Florida State University. Prior to assuming this position in 2014, he served in a number of roles within the College of Visual Arts, Theatre, and Dance, including associate dean, chair of the department of art, and interim dean. He also worked in the College of Family and Consumer Sciences and the Career Center at the University of Georgia. He earned his PhD in higher education administration from Bowling Green State University, his MA in journalism and ABJ in public relations from the University of Georgia, and his AS in accounting from South Georgia College. Hogan is active in the Commission for Academic Affairs in ACPA: College Student Educators International and has served as chair, cochair, and historian. He received the commission's award for Service to the Commission and ACPA in 2005. He has published and presented on topics such as client services in higher education, collaborations between academic and student affairs, and homophobia and AIDS in higher education.

ADRIANNA KEZAR is professor of higher education at the University of Southern California and codirector of the Pullias Center for Higher Education. Kezar is a national expert on change, governance, and leadership in higher education, and her research agenda explores the change process in higher education institutions and the role of leadership in creating change. She is well published, with 15 books, over 75 journal articles, and more than 100 book chapters and reports. Recent books include *Enhancing Campus Capacity for Leadership: An Examination of Grassroots Leaders in Higher Education* (Stanford University Press, 2011); *Understanding the New Majority of Non-Tenure Track Faculty: Demographics, Experiences, and Plans of Action* (Jossey-Bass, 2010); and *Organizing for Collaboration: A Guide for Campus Leaders* (Jossey-Bass, 2009).

AMBER RACCHINI is an instructor in the department of developmental studies at Indiana University of Pennsylvania and also the coordinator for supplemental instruction and peer assistance. She earned an EdD in 2010 and an MA in 2003 from Indiana University of Pennsylvania. She has worked in a variety of student affairs positions in residence life, orientation, disability support services, and student conduct. More recently, she began teaching in the first-year experience program that targets at-risk students. The focus of her research includes examining persistence, retention, and time to degree attainment for at-risk students. She has presented on this topic at the Pennsylvania Association of Developmental Education, Pennsylvania College Personnel Association (PCPA), and Undergraduate Advising Conference at Pennsylvania State University. She has served the professional community by serving in various roles on the executive board for PCPA.

KORINE STEINKE WAWRZYNSKI is the assistant dean for academic initiatives and director for undergraduate research in the provost's office at Michigan State University. She also serves as an adjunct assistant professor in the student affairs administration master's degree program. Wawrzynski is an active member of the Council on Undergraduate Research, where she serves as a councillor, and has cochaired two national conferences. She is also active with the Commission for Academic Affairs in ACPA: College Educators International and served as its chair. Her research interests include innovative learning opportunities for undergraduate students, the experiences of women leaders in higher education, and collaborative partnerships between academic affairs and student affairs. She earned a bachelor's degree in English from Monmouth College and a master's degree in college student personnel and a doctorate in higher education administration from Bowling Green State University.

Index

for LGBTQ students, 73
for lower social class backgrounds,
    72–73
for multiple identities, 74–75
for women, 70
admissions, 22
adults, 69
adult student services, 25
advising sessions, 20, 52–53
American Association for Higher
    Education, 94, 97
American Association of University
    Professors, 14
American College Personnel
    Association, 18–19
American Council on Education,
    14–15

Baxter Magolda, Marcia, 49–50,
    54–55, 124–25
border studies, 5

campus activities, 21, 22
campus counseling services, 27–28, 56
career counseling, 56
career exploration, 122–23
career fairs, 24
career paths, x–xi, 122–23
career services, 23–24
Chickering, Arthur
    on career counseling, 56
    on curriculum design, 54
    on identity aspects, 62
    on psychosocial model, 38–39
    on undergraduate research, 121–23
citizenship education, 96
cognitive complexity, 54, 100
cognitive development
    cognitive-structural model of, 40–43,
        124
    for diversity initiatives, 54–55
    moral development and, 45

in undergraduate research, 123–25
cognitive development, in
    undergraduate research, 123
    duration and complexity results for,
        125
    self-authorship in, 124–25
    stages of, 124
cognitive reasoning. See cognitive
    development
cognitive science, 40–43, 45, 54–55,
    123–25
cognitive spectrum, 124–25
cognitive-structural model
    dualism in, 40–41, 124
    King and Kitchener on, 42–43
    Piaget and, 40
    for undergraduate research, 124
collaboration, xii–xiv, 5–6, 104
    for academic honor, 113–17
    barriers to, 2–3
    cultural change strategies for, 6
    fictional account of, 89–91
    lack of, 1
    for military-affiliated students, 76
    need for, 1–2
    success characteristics for, 101–103
collaboration, academic affairs
        challenges
    discipline and division crossing as,
        93, 95
    hierarchical administrative structures
        as, 92–94
    historical division as, 95–96
    individualistic reward systems as, 94
    methodology differences as, 95
    unfamiliarity as, 94–95
collaboration, areas for
    first-year experience seminars as,
        96–97
    in institutional environments, 5–6
    institutional type and, 96
    learning communities as, 97

remuneration as, 128
research mentor as, 126, 130–31
structure as, 127
student qualifications as, 127–28
undergraduate research, personal
    development through
career path clarification in, 122–23
independence and interdependence
    in, 122
interpersonal competence in, 121–22
undergraduate research, student
    development results, 120
for cognitive development, 123–25
for personal development, 121–23
undergraduate research grants, 130

travel grants as, 131–33
undergraduate research journals, 133
university life, 1

value of education, 67
veteran and military-affiliated students.
    See military-affiliated and veteran
    students
veteran services, 76

women, 69–70
    dean of, 13
women's student services, 25–26

Zhao, C. M., 4–5

Also available from Stylus

Student Affairs Assessment
Theory to Practice

Gavin W. Henning and Darby Roberts

Foreword by Marilee J. Bresciani Ludvik

With the recognition of the integral role of student affairs in student education, and with stakeholders requiring increasing accountability at a time of tight resources, it has become imperative that staff be familiar with and competent in undertaking assessment. This book provides student affairs staff with the grounding they need to integrate assessment into how they design and monitor the programs, services, and activities they create to contribute to students' development.

This book is intended both as a text for student affairs and higher education master's programs and as a practical guide for early career staff who have had little formal preparation in assessment. It can be used for self-study or in professional development workshops. For divisions, departments, or units getting started with assessment, the discussion questions at the end of the chapters can engage staff in the process of developing an effective assessment culture.

This book provides a thorough introduction to all aspects of assessment, assuming no prior knowledge, and is illustrated throughout with examples of application in student affairs settings.

"Rigor in implementing assessment is emphasized throughout this volume. Rigor also characterizes the book's contents, which are particularly thorough in explaining why and how to do assessment and how to use results to improve programs and services. The authors make unique contributions in chapters on epistemology, politics, closing the loop, and ethics."—*Trudy W. Banta, Professor of Higher Education and Senior Advisor to the Chancellor, Indiana University–Purdue University Indianapolis*

22883 Quicksilver Drive
Sterling, VA 20166-2102

Subscribe to our e-mail alerts: www.Styluspub.com